I0015070

# Cloud Computing

## A Brief Introduction to Cloud Computing

*(The Ultimate Guide to Amazon Web Services – Cloud Computing)*

**Donald Wilson**

Published By **Oliver Leish**

# Donald Wilson

*Cloud Computing: A Brief Introduction to Cloud Computing (The Ultimate Guide to Amazon Web Services – Cloud Computing)*

ISBN  978-1-7770981-1-7

No part of this guidebook shall be reproduced in any form without permission in writing from the publisher except in the case of brief quotations embodied in critical articles or reviews.

Legal & Disclaimer

The information contained in this book is not designed to replace or take the place of any form of medicine or professional medical advice. The information in this book has been provided for educational & entertainment purposes only.

The information contained in this book has been compiled from sources deemed reliable, and it is accurate to the best of the Author's knowledge; however, the Author cannot guarantee its accuracy and validity and cannot be held liable for any errors or omissions. Changes are periodically made to this book. You must consult your doctor or get professional medical advice before using any of the suggested remedies, techniques, or information in this book.

Table Of Contents

## Chapter 1: Before Cloud Computing

Conventional business applications are costly and problematic. The assortment and amount of software and hardware needed to operate them were overwhelming. Companies required an entire team of specialists to operate, protect, modify, set up, analyze, install, and configure them. When this effort is multiplied across numerous applications, it becomes clear to see why it was difficult for small and midsize companies to get customized solutions. This was only possible for larger companies with great IT departments. Improvements in cloud computing have transformed that. Cloud computing has eradicated or restructured many of the features associated with setting up traditional IT infrastructure:

•Earlier, employees had to email documents back and forth; where at a time, there would be multiple versions of a document saved locally on numerous devices as well as occurrences of employees making changes to their version of the document. Files stored in the cloud with shared permissions are always current, there can be assurance that all employees are working on the same file with similar information.

•There was always the fear that a natural disaster or an emergency could destroy all the records of a company, since information saved physically in the company's computers is susceptible to failure or loss. Information saved in the cloud has several more protections.

•Updates to software used to entail huge expenses after some years, in order to acquire the most recent version of essential programs. There was manual application installation and maintenance on every device. Only the major organizations could employ software developers to develop custom-made software. Security issues and defects might not be resolved for a long time.

•A specific geographic work location can no longer hinder an employee's access to information and processes; with the cloud, they can work remotely and still be as productive.

•Physically backing up data on discs, hard drives, or other devices is no longer necessary.

•Even though technology professionals are still sought after by companies, there is no longer a need for specialized experts to troubleshoot software and hardware systems, as monotonous activities like installing updates on computers one after another have been removed.

•Companies no longer have to store groups of servers in equipment rooms or airy closets.

Misunderstandings about Cloud Computing

Some companies might be hesitant about the shift from legacy, in-house systems or applications to an entirely cloud-based infrastructure. Several concerns regarding the cloud are due to common, sometimes outdated misconceptions. Some of these are noted below:

•Cloud systems are not secure

Some technical and operational executives are worried that the cloud is not safe or at a minimum not as safe as the in-house systems. The significance for security in businesses today cannot be overstated, so these executives have the right to be vigilant. Bearing in mind the delicate nature of client data that companies save, particularly financial or personal information, it is rational that technology experts want to have thorough assurance in the infrastructures they depend on. With that understood, it is important to note that while in-house infrastructures maintain data within the company's firewall, it does not denote that it is resistant to threats. A good example of this would be the Equifax breach in 2017.

In many instances, the cloud is safer than in-house systems because of the cloud provider's commitment to and focus on continuous security procedures. Not only do cloud providers have assigned in-house resources, they also frequently depend on external inspections to preserve certifications and compliance, and help clients in validating security processes and policies. They utilize several industry standards like Federal Risk and Authorization Management Program (FedRAMP), Service Organization Controls 2 (SOC2), Health Insurance Portability & Accountability Act (HIPAA), General Data Protection Regulation (GDPR), or Payment Card Industry (PCI). The cloud provider's operation is reliant on security, uptime and dependability. For example, big cloud-based facilities such as Office 365 and G Suite are reinforced by systems that regularly installs patches and updates, which aids regulate security threats. This liberates the company from the burden of handling the entire security of the systems and installing updates.

However, companies should know that there is no business that is wholly protected from security breaches irrespective of their system architecture. Security is typically still the company's obligation after moving across the physical layer. There is the requirement to make certain that the data is encrypted at all times, security groups and network ACLs are organized, and servers' operating systems are safe. Cloud computing makes this easier to accomplish, since the tools to complete a number of these fundamental tasks are sometimes already included, or easily accessible as an add-on to other services — that would have been more expensive or more problematic otherwise. Businesses that make intelligent decisions regarding their architecture, may transfer the responsibility of several modules to a cloud provider through the utilization of regulated services. One good example for the occasion where the management of the operating system is no longer the company's is RDS for databases.

•Absence of appropriate encryption in the cloud

Many people get the wrong idea about the implementation of encryption to maintain data securely. For instance, encryption is mostly utilized for data-in-transit, where data is safeguarded against been seen from anyone as it moves from a particular internet address to a different one. However, data-at-rest can also be encrypted, where data stored in a system is encrypted. Considering this, a company have to know the form of encryption it needs. When it is time to select the suitable cloud service, it would be good to know about the security processes that a cloud architecture executes and determine how it can guard the company's data.

•Intermingling of client data in multi-tenant cloud systems

When a company seeks some services of a cloud provider, they turn out to be one of numerous clients, with all existing on the same cloud infrastructure. This led to a worry that data is getting mixed up, that data in one company is visible to other companies on the same infrastructure, and that on the premise that a single account is hacked it's simple to gain entrance to a different company's sensitive client data. This does not apply to cloud-native resources. Cloud providers makes major effort to guarantee that hosted data is only accessible by the company that owns it; thus, their software infrastructures are purposely developed to certify that. Additionally, inserting new customers to the infrastructure is really an advantage to existing tenants. Since it is easier for the cloud provider to comprehend network activities and augment performance preemptively when there is more data to work with.

•Companies are no more accountable for data security when on the cloud

Even though cloud security is vital, safeguarding data eventually depends on the consumers with access. Losing unlocked business mobile phones or computers can leave data exposed and undermine the company's whole cloud architecture. That is why it is suggested to always have robust verification techniques ready for devices used to gain entrance to the cloud.

•The cloud is never out of order

Similar to other technological resources, cloud-based resources are not resistant to technical problems. For instance, some cloud providers have experienced server failures and outages that damaged files and possibly data loss in the process. An additional cause of failure for cloud services is hacking. Utilizing a cloud service that is not optimal and is susceptible to attacks can result in deleted or stolen data, which can be difficult to recover if there are no offline backups. It is necessary to clarify with a cloud provider about the guaranteed features, before committing to any form of cloud service. Several cloud providers make assurances concerning a service's safety or its uptime for provider-connected breaches.

How Cloud Computing Works

Cloud computing consist of two features backend and frontend. Frontend is the user-facing aspect of the cloud involving user interactions. It encompasses applications and interfaces that are essential to gain entrance to the cloud infrastructure. Whereas backend includes the software and hardware that are needed for cloud computing operations. This consists of security mechanisms, data storage, servers, virtual machines, etc. The cloud provider manages it. The backend is responsible for managing data security, traffic control and regulating protocols.

Each application in the cloud has a host, the cloud provider is tasked with sustaining the huge datacenters that offer the computing power, storage capacity, and security required to retain every information sent by the users to the cloud. Cloud providers can sell the privileges to utilize their clouds as well as save data on their systems, while also presenting to the customer an environment for interconnection between programs and devices.

## Chapter 2: Types of Cloud Computing

There are three types of cloud computing, commonly referred to as Software-as-a-Service (SaaS), Platform-as-a-Service (PaaS), and Infrastructure-as-a-Service (IaaS). Choosing the appropriate type of cloud computing needed, can assist in striking the right amount of control and avoid undifferentiated heavy lifting.

•Software-as-a-Service (SaaS)

This refers to a method for distributing software, wherein a service provider or vendor hosts applications which are made available to clients over the internet. Through multitenant architecture, SaaS strictly offers business software to tons of customers. All the elements that describe a software, from algorithms, codes, and scripts, along with the physical hardware (in terms of the structures and servers that store them) are retained and maintained by the providers in their own facilities. SaaS is turning out to be an increasingly predominant delivery model and an underlying technology that supports Web Services or Service Oriented Architecture (SOA). Via the internet, this solution is available to users everywhere. Previously, software application was required to be purchased upfront, after which it is installed on the computer. On the other hand, SaaS users pay for subscriptions to the software instead of purchasing it. Some SaaS solutions are offered free, but many entail an annual or monthly subscription to retain the service. Requiring no management or hardware installation, SaaS solutions are very successful in the business world. Many important tasks such as planning, invoicing, sales, and accounting can be carried out using SaaS.

SaaS deployment model

This has to do with the way cloud providers use the internet to distribute software and bill their users, who simply run the software on the browsers of their mobile devices or computers—all the software being managed by the provider's servers. This multi-tenant, provider-hosted processing and server model is the opposite of the traditional on-site model of deploying software. The low barrier to implementation of this model has encouraged trial and freemium opportunities through which most users originally experience the product. Because of its web delivery format, SaaS eliminates the requirement to download and install software on each individual computer, which is not a pleasant prospect for any IT staff. Providers manage all of the possible technical issues such as storage, servers, middleware, and data, while companies can simply streamline their support and maintenance.

The deployment model of SaaS is comparable to the establishment stage of a utility amenity, which is followed by billing and metering at regular interims for the amenities that have been provided. A SaaS provider through a user provisioning procedure, which is often automated, typically initiates SaaS deployment. Consecutively, a third-party-managed (hosted) services vendor can initiate

SaaS deployment. SaaS deployment is regarded as complete as soon as a user has the required method to access a SaaS solution, irrespective of whether the user starts using the service after it has been provisioned.

Characteristics of SaaS

Below are some ways to aid in determining when SaaS is being used:

•Users not responsible for software or hardware updates.

•Administered from a central location.

•Easily reached over the internet.

•Hosted on a virtual server by an external provider.

•Inclusive, offering maintenance, compliance, and security as part of the fee.

•Scalable, with diverse tiers for large, medium and small businesses.

•The capacity for each user to simply customize applications to accommodate their business processes without having an effect on the common infrastructure. Due to the way SaaS is built, these customizations are distinct to each user or company and are always preserved via upgrades. Meaning that SaaS vendors can make upgrades more frequently, with much lower adoption cost and less customer risk.

•A multitenant architecture, where all applications and users share a particular, common code base and infrastructure that is centrally maintained. Since customers for SaaS providers are all on similar code base and infrastructure, providers can innovate more rapidly and save the valued development time formerly spent on maintaining various versions of outdated code.

When to utilize SaaS

SaaS is an appropriate option for the following:

•For applications that require both mobile and web access.

•A small company or startup that desires to launch ecommerce rapidly, with limited time or resources for resolving server issues.

•For short-term projects necessitating collaboration.

•Applications with inconsistent demand, such as tax software.

Benefits of using SaaS

The essential benefits of SaaS include:

•Access application data from everywhere. Users can access their stored in the cloud from any mobile device or computer connected to the internet. Moreover, data is not lost when a user's device or computer fails, since the data is saved in the cloud.

•Easily mobilize employees. With SaaS, it is easier for companies to mobilize employees, since users can access SaaS data and applications from any mobile device or computer connected to the internet. There is no concern about developing applications to run on various types of devices and computers because the service vendor has already done this. Additionally, there is no need to bring an expert onboard to handle the security problems inherent in cloud computing. A carefully selected service provider will guarantee the security of users' data, irrespective of the kind of device consuming it.

•Users can work on most SaaS applications through their web browser without having to download and set up any software, although some applications require plugins. This indicates that a company does not need to procure and install any special software for its users.

•Easy scalability. Payment is made for only what is utilized, thus saving money since the SaaS solution automatically scales down and up based on the level of usage. That is particularly important for companies whose operations are cyclical in nature, and also for companies that are growing quickly.

•SaaS makes even advanced enterprise applications, like CRM and ERP, affordable for companies that don't have the resources to purchase, deploy, and manage the necessary software and infrastructure themselves.

•SaaS customers also take advantage of the fact that service vendors can set up automatic updates in software—mostly on a monthly or weekly basis—so companies do not have to be concerned about installing patches like security updates, or purchasing new releases when they are available. This can be particularly appealing to companies with inadequate IT staff to manage these tasks.

Disadvantages of SaaS

SaaS comes with some challenges and risks that companies should be aware of to capitalize on the advantages of the delivery model. These are:

•Downtime and performance. Since the provider manages and controls the SaaS service, customers rely on providers to maintain performance and security of the service. Network issues, cyber-attacks or unplanned and planned maintenance may affect the performance of the application in spite of adequate Service Level Agreement (SLA) defenses in place.

•Limited modules. Since SaaS applications sometimes come in a standardized format, the choice of modules may be a compromise against performance, cost, security, or other organizational policies. Besides, due to the security, cost or vendor lock-in fears, it may not be feasible to switch services or vendors to serve new feature requests in the future.

•Lack of control. SaaS services effectively involves turning over controls to the external service vendor. These controls are not restricted to the software – with regard to the appearance, updates or version– but also the governance and data. Consequently, customers may have to redefine their data governance and security models to fit the functionality and features of the SaaS service.

•Customization. SaaS applications offer very little capability for customization. Since there is no one-size-fits-all solution, users may be restricted to specific integrations, performance and functionality as offered by the provider. On the other hand, on-site solutions that come with various software development kits offer a wide range of customization options.

•Data security. There may be a need to transfer large amount of data to the remote datacenters of SaaS applications with the intention of performing necessary software operations. Transferring sensitive business data to public-cloud dependent SaaS solution may compromise compliance and security, in addition to incurring significant cost in transferring large data workloads.

•Lack of integration support: Several companies want deep integrations with on-site services, data and applications. The SaaS provider may offer inadequate support in this matter, forcing companies to use internal resources for managing and designing integrations. The difficulty of integrations can further restrict how the SaaS application or other related services can be utilized.

•Vendor lock-In. Providers may make it very simple to register and acquire a service but difficult to withdraw. For example, it may require internal engineering rework or incur significant cost to transfer SaaS applications from other providers. Not all providers follow standard tools, protocols, and APIs, yet the features offered could be essential for certain business tasks.

•Interoperability. Integration with existing services and applications can be a huge concern if the SaaS application is not built to comply with available standards for integration. In that event, companies may have to minimize dependencies with SaaS services or build their own integration systems, which is probably not possible all the time.

Popular SaaS solutions

There are so many SaaS solutions available in the market today. Below are some of the well-known ones:

•Slack

A real-time search, archiving and messaging solution, Slack is readdressing business communication. Users may establish team discussions in open channels assigned to specific projects or topics, or limit more sensitive discussions to private, invite-only members. Colleagues also may converse one-on-one by making use of private, protected direct messages. Slack also allows users to share PDFs, spreadsheets, documents and files, complete with options for highlighting and inserting comments for future reference; moreover, all files, notifications and messages are automatically indexed and archived.

•Dropbox

Using Dropbox, users are able to keep documents and files at close reach across all devices. Whatever is inserted into Dropbox storage automatically appears across all mobile and desktop devices, facilitating professionals to start a project on their computer at work, make changes on their smartphone when going home, and add the final edits from their home tablet. Users can also ask coworkers to access a particular Dropbox folder or forward specific images and files accessible via password-protected links; there is an additional remote wipe choice in case of emergency.

•Google Apps

For a while now, Google has expanded beyond its advertising and search roots to offer companies a wide-ranging sets of productivity tools. This comprises of Google Drive, shared video meetings and calendars, as well as custom professional email (including spam protection). Google Drive is a document storage solution based in the cloud, that allows users to access documents from any system and share them directly with coworkers, in the process removing email attachments along with the hassles of merging several versions.

•Salesforce.com

Perhaps, the ideal SaaS application, Salesforce stays at the frontline of the cloud computing transformation it helped build. The customer relations management product empowers businesses to gather all information on leads, prospects and customers in a single online platform, permitting authorized employees to access sensitive data on any connected system at any time. Salesforce gives credit to its tools for increasing customer sales to about 37 percent in addition to driving increased customer satisfaction and loyalty.

•Microsoft Office 365

Popular Microsoft productivity applications like PowerPoint, Excel and Word are longstanding staples of the workplace;

however, Microsoft Office 365 that is based in the cloud dramatically magnifies the Office suite's parameters. With it, users can create, edit and share files from any Windows, Android, iOS, Mac or PC device in real-time, interact with customers and colleagues across a variety of tools from video conferencing to email and leverage an assortment of collaborative technologies assisting secure interactions both outside and inside of the company.

•Zendesk

This cloud-based support ticketing and customer service platform allows representatives to more efficiently handle inbound client demands across any communications channel —chat, phone, social media, web or email. Features include Zendesk Voice (a cloud-based, integrated phone support solution), Zopim (a real-time chat solution) and Automatic Answers (a tool powered by machine learning for solving and interpreting customer requests and questions). As stated by Zendesk, its business users receive positive ratings for over 86 percent of interactions with their customers.

•DocuSign

This is a transaction management services and electronic signature technology platform that supports the transfer of digital contracts as well as other e-signed files. Users may read, sign and submit business documents from any location, guaranteeing agreements and approvals are executed in minutes, instead of days. DocuSign e-signatures are considered to be legally binding for most personal and business relations in virtually every country across the globe.

•Amazon Web Services

Amazon has also transformed beyond its main e-commerce platform to assist the on-demand delivery of IT applications and resources based in the cloud, reinforced by pay-as-you-go pricing choices. Currently, Amazon Web Services has more than 70 services, including resources for the Internet of Things, management, deployment, analytics, database, networking, storage, and computing.

•Box

This virtual workspace allows professionals to work together with anyone, anywhere. Customers can securely share huge files through custom URL or traditional link, safeguarding documents and data through password protection and permissions. Box supports over 120 file types, and customers may preview content before downloading. All content approval, discussion, editing and sharing is confined to a single centralized file, and customers receive real-time notifications when changes are made. Additionally, Box automates tasks like contract approvals and employee onboarding, reducing repetition and shortening review cycles.

•Platform-as-a-Service (PaaS)

PaaS has to do with cloud computing services that support the development and deployment of web applications. PaaS supports the entire lifecycle of applications, assisting users in building, testing, deploying, managing and updating all in one location — without the complexity and cost of purchasing and management of the underlying software and hardware. The service also includes infrastructure, database management, operating systems, business intelligence solutions, middleware and development tools.

PaaS delivery

There is similarity between the delivery model of SaaS and PaaS, except, rather than providing the software through the internet, PaaS delivers a platform for creating software. This platform is delivered through the web, allowing developers to fully concentrate on developing the software without getting concerned about the infrastructure, storage, software updates or operating systems. PaaS allows businesses to create and design applications that are integrated into the PaaS with distinctive software components. These middleware or applications, are highly available and scalable as they adopt certain cloud characteristics.

Characteristics of PaaS

Here are some key features of PaaS model:

•Facilitates collaborative work even when teams work remotely.

•Databases and web services are integrated.

•Several users can retrieve the same development application.

•It is established on virtualization technology, signifying that resources can simply be scaled down or up according to business changes.

•Offers an assortment of services to help with developing, testing, and deploying applications.

When to utilize PaaS

PaaS is an appropriate option for modern application Development. If there are several developers engaged in the same development task, or if other providers must also be included, PaaS can offer great flexibility and speed to the whole process. PaaS is also helpful if there is need to create customized applications. It can greatly minimize costs and it can rectify some challenges that arise when speedily developing or deploying an application.

Benefits of PaaS:

•Efficiently control the application lifecycle. PaaS offers all of the abilities that is needed to support the entire web application lifecycle: development, testing, deployment, management, and maintenance inside the same integrated environment.

•Support development teams that are in different locations. Since the internet is used to access the development environment, teams can still collaborate on projects despite the locations of team members.

•Use sophisticated tools inexpensively. A pay-as-you-go system makes it possible for businesses or individuals to use business analytics and intelligence tools and sophisticated development software that they could not manage to purchase outright.

•Develop for several platforms—including mobile—more simply. Some service vendors give development options for several platforms, like browsers, mobile devices, and computers making cross-platform applications easier and faster to develop.

•Add development capacity without adding staff. PaaS features can give development teams new capacity without having to add staff with the required skills.

•Reduce coding time. PaaS development solutions can reduce the time used to develop new applications with pre-coded application features built into the platform, for example search, security features, directory services, workflow, and so on.

•Facilitates easy movement to the hybrid model.

•Automates business policy.

•Minimize complications by using middleware as a service.

Disadvantages of PaaS

The concerns and limitations of PaaS include:

•Operational restriction. Custom-built cloud-based operations administration and automation workflows are probably not applicable to PaaS resources as the platform usually restricts operational capabilities for end-users. Even though this is intended to lessen the operational burden on users, the loss of operational power may influence how PaaS solutions are operated, provisioned and managed.

•Customization of outdated systems: PaaS is probably not a plug-and-play resolution for existing legacy services and applications. Numerous configuration changes and customizations may be necessary for outdated systems to function with the PaaS solution. The resulting customization may produce a complicated IT system that may restrict the worth of the PaaS investment completely.

•Runtime problems: Other than the restrictions associated with specific services and applications, PaaS deliverables may not be augmented for the frameworks and language needed by a company. Specific framework versions are either not available or do not perform excellently with the PaaS solution, thus development of custom dependencies with the framework will be limited.

•Vendor lock-In. Technical and business requirements that direct decision for a particular PaaS solution may not be utilized in the future. If the provider has not provisioned appropriate migration policies, switching to another PaaS provider may not be likely without affecting the business.

•Integrations: There is an increase in the complexity of integrating the data stored inside in-house datacenter or off-site cloud, and it may affect which services and applications can be implemented with the PaaS offering. Particularly when not every feature of an outdated IT system is developed for the cloud, integrating with existing infrastructure and services may be a challenge.

•Data security: Even though companies can run their own services and applications using PaaS resources, the data residing in external cloud servers controlled by providers poses security concerns and risks. The security choices may also be inadequate as users are probably not able to use services with specific hosting procedures.

Popular PaaS solutions

Among the leading PaaS vendors are Heroku, Engine Yard, Mendix, Pivotal, Red Hat, Salesforce.com, IBM, Google, Microsoft, and Amazon Web Services (AWS). Most widely used containers, libraries, languages, and associated tools are available on every major PaaS vendors' clouds. Google, Microsoft, and Amazon in particular offer complete collections of cloud-based solutions including security, management tools, developer tools, mobile backend, networking, analytics, databases, storage, and computing tools. In many situations, these wholly managed services supplement the PaaS solutions in these public clouds. It is no coincidence that many PaaS providers are also leading vendors of software development tools.

Here is a short introduction to some of the popular PaaS offerings:

•Pivotal Cloud Foundry

This is an open source solution managed through the Cloud Foundry Foundation. Cloud Foundry was initially created by VMware and then moved to Pivotal Software, a collaborative venture by General Electric, VMWare, and EMC. Cloud Foundry is developed for running and building container-based applications, making use of Kubernetes for orchestration.

•OpenShift by Red Hat

OpenShift is a collection of PaaS solutions, which can be deployed on-site or cloud-hosted, for deploying and building containerized applications. The leading resource is the OpenShift Container Platform, which is an on-site PaaS developed around Docker containers that are managed and orchestrated by Kubernetes with Red Hat Enterprise Linux as the foundation.

•Microsoft Azure Functions

This can be referred to as a serverless computing framework that allows developers to operate by connecting to messaging solutions or data sources, making it easy to react and process events. Developers can utilize Azure Functions to develop HTTP-based API endpoints easily reached through a range of applications.

•Microsoft Azure App Service

This is a completely managed PaaS that integrates BizTalk Services, Mobile Services, and Microsoft Azure Websites into one offering. Azure App Service offers integration between cloud and on-site systems.

•Google Cloud Functions

This is created to make it simple for developers to scale and run code in the cloud in addition to building event-driven serverless applications.

•Google App Engine

This is a PaaS solution for hosting and developing web applications in datacenters managed by Google. Applications are automatically sandboxed, run, and scaled over multiple servers.

•AWS Lambda

This serverless, event-driven computing framework runs specified code in response to incidents, and automatically handles the computing resources required by that code.

AWS Lambda made the FaaS concept popular, although it predates the term.

•AWS Elastic Beanstalk

Using this offering, companies can rapidly manage and deploy applications that are hosted in the AWS Cloud without needing to learn about the framework that controls the applications. This solution automatically handles the specifics of application health monitoring, scaling, load balancing, and capacity provisioning.

•Infrastructure-as-a-Service (IaaS)

IaaS offers on-demand access to computing infrastructure. This includes resources like compute, networks and storage that is required to run workloads. The collection of hardware resources is retrieved from multiple networks and servers usually distributed across several datacenters. This provides reliability and redundancy to IaaS. A user can request computing services when needed and pay for only what is consumed. IaaS vendors supply a virtual server storage and instance, along with APIs that allow users to transfer workloads to a virtual machine. Users have an assigned storage capacity and can access, configure, stop and start the virtual machine and storage as preferred. IaaS vendors provides small, medium, large, extra-large as well as compute-optimized or memory-optimized instances, along with customized instances, for several workload needs. IaaS delivers the highest level of management control and flexibility over computing resources and is very similar to current IT resources that several IT developers and departments are familiar with today.

IaaS delivery

IaaS delivers cloud computing infrastructure via virtualization technology. These cloud resources are usually provided to the company through an API or a dashboard, and IaaS clients have full control over the whole infrastructure. IaaS offers the same capabilities and technologies as a conventional datacenter without physically maintaining or managing all of it. IaaS customers can still access their storage and servers directly, but this is now outsourced through a cloud-based datacenter.

Different from PaaS or SaaS, IaaS clients have the responsibility of managing features such as data, middleware, operating systems, runtime, and applications. However, IaaS vendors manage the storage, virtualization, networking, hard drives, and servers. Some vendors even provide more services apart from the virtualization layer, for example message queuing or databases.

Characteristics of IaaS

Here are some key features of IaaS model:

•Flexible and dynamic.

•Gives full control of the platform to companies.

•Normally includes several users on one piece of hardware.

•Services are greatly scalable.

•The cost differs depending on consumption.

•Resources are accessible as a service.

•GUI and API-based access.

•Platform virtualization technology.

•Automated administrative tasks.

When to utilize IaaS

IaaS is a great option for a small company or a startup since there's no need to spend money or time trying to create software and hardware. IaaS is also advantageous for large companies that desire to have full control over their infrastructures and applications, but only want to purchase what is actually needed or consumed. For companies that are growing quickly, IaaS can be a worthy option since they do not have to be tied to a specific software or hardware as their requirements evolve and change. IaaS also helps if there is uncertainty about the demands a different application will need, as there is enough flexibility to scale down or up as needed.

Benefits of IaaS

•Decrease wasted resources. Transparent metering, pricing, and chargeback tools enable IT administrators to identify where costs can be decreased.

•Quick scalability. Instantly distribute new computing resources to satisfy business demands because of peak periods, company decline or growth.

•Better agility. Computing resources can be supplied on demand and sent back to the resource pool simply.

•Greater efficiency. Resources are pooled and virtualized ensuring physical infrastructure is utilized to maximum capacity.

•Improved security. With the proper service agreement, vendors can offer security for data and applications that may be superior to what can be attained in-house.

•Increased supportability, dependability, and stability. With IaaS, it is not required to maintain and upgrade hardware and software or troubleshoot equipment issues. With the right agreement established, the service provider guarantees that a company's infrastructure is dependable and meets service level agreement (SLA).

•Innovate quickly. As soon as the decision has been made to launch a new initiative or product, the essential computing infrastructure can be prepared in minutes or hours, instead of the longer length of time it could take to build internally.

## Chapter 3: Cloud deployment models

Below are the forms of cloud deployment models:

•Public cloud

This form of cloud is typically utilized for Business to Consumer (B2C) related interactions. Cloud service providers manage and own public clouds, while distributing their computing resources, such as commercial infrastructure environments or operating system platform (utilized for testing and software development, storage, servers, applications, virtual machines) through the internet. Services offered could be free or provided via a number of subscription or by-request pricing arrangements, as well as a pay-per-usage format. Users only make payment for the bandwidth, storage or CPU cycles they consume. The public cloud provides a huge array of computing resources and solutions to handle the rising requirements of companies of all verticals and sizes.

How public cloud works

A public cloud has an entirely virtualized infrastructure. Cloud providers develop a multi-tenant infrastructure that allows tenants or users to have common computing resources. However, every user's data remains inaccessible to other users. It also depends on high transmission capacity of network connections for quick data transfer. Storage on public cloud is usually redundant, making use of several datacenters and duplication of file versions. Due to this, it has earned a reputation for flexibility.

A public cloud is possibly the easiest out of the other cloud deployments models: A user demanding more services, platforms or resources, basically pays the provider by the byte or hour to have the right to use needed services on-demand. Cloud-based applications, storage, raw processing power or infrastructure are gotten remotely from hardware maintained by the provider, combined into data groups, coordinated by automation and management software, and transferred through the internet to the user. The users do not possess the tons of storage they utilize; do not administer procedures at the server farm hosting the hardware; and do not regulate the maintenance or security of their cloud-based services, applications, or platforms. Public cloud consumers merely assent to an arrangement, utilize the services offered, and make payment for needed resources.

Public cloud characteristics

The main characteristics of public clouds are:

•The cloud provider administers the virtualization software, provisions the network and preserves the hardware beneath the cloud.

•Distribution of resources could be free or on-demand.

•Tenants within the cloud provider's firewall have common virtual resources and cloud services that are gotten from the cloud provider's group of software, platforms and infrastructure.

•Facilitates dynamic PaaS for deployment environments and application development in the cloud.

•Enablement for accessible, flexible IaaS for compute and storage services instantaneously.

•Provides access to inventive SaaS commercial applications for applications extending from data analytics and transaction administration to customer resource management (CRM).

Public cloud use cases

The public cloud is an appropriate option for the following:

•Test environments and software development.

•Supplementary resource requests to tackle fluctuating peak demands.

•Services and applications required to carry out business and IT operations.

•Anticipated computing requirements, for example communication solutions for a particular number of users.

Benefits of public cloud

The essential benefits of public clouds include:

•Minimized complexity and requirements on technical proficiency, since the cloud provider has the responsibility of handling the infrastructure.

•The cost savings enables companies to pursue lean growth approaches and concentrate investments on revolutionary projects.

•Less wasted resources as users only make payment for what they utilize.

•Cost effectiveness. Developing a private cloud can get very costly. There is a need to contemplate the original fee to purchase every hardware required, and then the continuing upkeep, comprising of the manpower or technical experts, the improvement sequence as equipment gets to end-of-life, and hardware failures. A public cloud replaces this with an agreement for a recurrent fee that offers the above without the expensive startup charge. With bigger cloud providers, there are economies of scale, as they host numerous accounts, thus can buy and operate equipment more competently, and at a reduced rate than several companies can achieve independently.

•Great dependability. The datacenter of most companies is located in a certain geographic site, which may be susceptible to power outages, disastrous weather occurrences, and other probable problems. Only a small percentage of companies have the means to create many datacenters, in many different geographic locations. Nevertheless, when it comes to public cloud, providers like Google and Microsoft are huge operations offering a massive system of servers through countless different parts, offering redundancy, and consequently a greater level of dependability, than most companies can offer independently. If there is an occurrence when one datacenter goes down, the rest would continue operating, and there would be no downtime experienced by the company.

•Scalability. Different from a private cloud, where companies must develop and create the infrastructure, a public cloud denotes the provider is responsible for offering the resources when required. An added advantage to the company is that this enables scaling of resources as desired, and to be alert to the intermittent rise in traffic that happen. For instance, this signifies that companies do not have to overpopulate their private cloud in order to handle an annual increase in demand.

Limitations of public cloud

The downsides to public cloud may include:

•Movement of data

A recurrent usage for public cloud is storing data remotely, capitalizing on redundancy to evade loss of data. However, issues can crop up when moving data as that will be dependent on internet speeds, plus the possibility of been hindered with congestion problems. In addition, the data can wind up in other countries, where it may be answerable to varying regulations and diverse data privacy laws.

•Reduced performance

Private cloud service connection is done through a faster corporate local area network, while public cloud is dependent on the internet connection. This can lead to increase in latency for applications, resulting in lesser performance, specifically since most datacenters can be situated quite far away geographically from their users.

•Security fears

Even though public cloud security has enhanced, there are still worries that servers shared with numerous consumers are characteristically not as secure as private cloud services committed to one company (with the possibility of added security behind the company's firewall). A current case in point of upsetting data leakages are the various 'bucket leaks' through Amazon Web Services from Accenture, GoDaddy, Tesla, and Spyfone.

Public cloud providers

There are tons of public cloud providers in the market, but the more popular ones are Google Cloud, Amazon Web Services, Alibaba Cloud and Microsoft Azure. These vendors offer their services through the internet, or via allocated connections, and utilize a central pay-per-usage method. Every vendor provides a collection of products focused on different enterprise needs and workloads. Some companies view the pay-per-usage method as a smart and more adaptable economic model. For instance, companies justify services acquired through public cloud as variable or operational cost instead of fixed or capital cost. In a few occasions, this indicates that companies do not need advanced budget arrangement or extensive reviews for public cloud choices. Despite that, since consumers usually set up public cloud solutions in a self-service method, a few organizations find it hard to correctly monitor cloud service utilizations, and possibly wind up paying for extra cloud solutions than is needed. Some companies also just have a preference to directly manage and supervise their own internal IT solutions, including servers.

•Private Cloud

This has to do with cloud computing solutions utilized entirely by a single company. It can be physically situated on the organization's internal datacenter. A few companies also request for the hosting of their private cloud by third-party vendors. The infrastructure and services in a private cloud are retained on a proprietary network. Private Cloud can also be known as on-premises cloud, internal cloud or corporate cloud.

A private cloud scales back the software utilized to operate IaaS public clouds into technologies that can be installed and run in a user's datacenter. Here, in-house clients can set up their own cloud resources to run, test and build applications, with measurements to bill departments for resource utilization. The private cloud aids administrators in the process of automating the datacenter, by reducing management and manual provisioning. Examples of private cloud providers include OpenStack and VMware. It is important to note that there is no full conformation of the private cloud to the description of cloud computing. A private cloud requires that a company develop and preserve its own core cloud framework; only the in-house consumers of a private cloud encounter that as a cloud computing solution.

Private cloud permits companies to profit from a few of the benefits of public cloud, without having to worry about surrendering control over services and data, since it is hidden behind the company's firewall. Businesses can control the location for data storage as well as develop their cloud framework as they want (mostly for PaaS or IaaS projects), to offer software developers entry to a collection of resources that scales as needed without jeopardizing security. On the other hand, that supplementary security does not come cheap, as some organizations will have the size and scope of Google, Microsoft or AWS, which suggests that they might not have the capacity to generate similar economies of scale. Regardless, for organizations that demand extra security, private cloud could be an important starting point, aiding in the comprehension of cloud solutions or restructuring in-house applications for deployment in the cloud, before been transferred to the public cloud.

How private cloud works

A private cloud utilizes virtualization to merge hardware resources into shared pools. With this method, there is no need for the cloud to build environments by virtualizing resources individually from a group of different physical infrastructures. An automated process can be configured to collect all required resources from one source. Inserting a layer of management application enables regulatory control over the data, applications, platforms, and infrastructure to be utilized in the cloud by assisting cloud administrators to recover or retain data, oversee integration points, and optimize and track use. By the time the last automation layer is inserted to reduce or replace human involvement with repeatable processes and instructions, the self-service aspect of the cloud is finalized, and that stack of technologies becomes a private cloud.

For a private cloud to function properly, automation, management and virtualization should be able to work well together. This would also depend on the operating system. The flexibility, dependability, and consistency of the operating system directly decides the strength of the connections between the users, automation scripts, virtual data pools, and physical resources. When that operating system is made freely available and developed for companies then the framework holding up the private cloud becomes not only dependable enough to act as a good foundation, but adaptable enough to scale.

Hosted private clouds

When a company sets up a private cloud, it is wholly responsible for every related cost as well as maintaining, managing, and staffing all underlying architecture. However, vendors can also deliver private clouds as part of a hosted private cloud strategy. Hosted private clouds allows clients to retain a private cloud — whether off or on premises—that is managed, configured, and deployed by a third-party provider. It is a cloud distribution option that assists companies with under-skilled or understaffed IT teams deliver improved private cloud infrastructure and services to users.

Private cloud characteristics

The main characteristics of private clouds are:

•Direct management of underlying cloud framework.

•In-house hardware.

•Single tenant framework.

•Resource pooling.

•Broad access. Phones, tablets, laptops, workstations and other devices can access resources stored in the cloud.

•On-demand self-service where users can provision resources without requesting for help from technical staff.

•Delivers sophisticated governance and security intended for a company's explicit requirements.

•Quick flexibility facilitates increasing or reducing capacity when required and freeing resources to be utilized by others when the requirement is fulfilled.

•Measured service assures that the users and the company can measure the amount of resources utilized, in order for those resources to be distributed in a way that optimizes their uses. These resources could be user accounts, bandwidth, processing and storage.

Private cloud use cases

The private cloud is an appropriate option for the following:

•Companies that have enough money to invest in high availability and performance technologies.

•Government agencies and highly regulated industries.

•Technology businesses that necessitate strong security and management over their technical functions and the underlying framework.

•Large companies that need innovative datacenter technologies to work proficiently and cost-effectively.

Benefits of a private cloud

The essential benefits of private clouds include:

•High SLA efficiency and performance.

•Improved visibility of infrastructural resources.

•Proficient resource provisioning based on needs of the users.

•Secure and dedicated environments that is not accessible by other companies.

•On-demand services by means of policy-based management and self-service user interfaces.

•Increased infrastructural capability to manage large storage and compute demands.

•High efficiency and scalability to meet unforeseeable demands without weakening performance and security.

•Flexibility to modify the framework based on ever-changing technical and business needs of the company. Private clouds can be completely configured by the company using the framework. An in-house cloud architect builds a completely private cloud. This means that stakeholders can describe the exact architecture required to run internal applications. Hosted private clouds provide similar benefits but does not need on-site installation. Therefore, the company works with a cloud provider to configure and manage a cloud for its private use.

•Compliance to strict regulations as companies can run measures, configurations and protocols to modify security based on distinct workload requests. For companies working in extremely regulated industries, compliance is vital. Private cloud framework offers companies the capability to comply

61

with stringent regulations since sensitive data is stored on hardware that is inaccessible outside the company. This benefit is available via hosted services as well as on-site hardware installations.

•Private clouds decrease occurrences of underutilized capacity. They enable companies to routinely configure and reconfigure resources as needed, since there is no restriction on the resources by their physical installations. Moreover, depending the company's security practices and policies, private clouds can deliver better security than other cloud models.

•When there is a requirement for extra computing resources, hybridization expands the solutions of the private cloud to that of public cloud to sustain productivity without having to set up extra physical servers. This will offer cost-effectiveness to companies that require the security provided by a private cloud but also want to take advantage of the benefits of a public cloud service.

Private cloud limitations

A private cloud can present problems if a company does not have predictable computing requirements. When the demand for resources is unstable, a private cloud might not be capable of scaling successfully, costing the company a lot of money in the end. The downsides to private cloud may include:

•When comparing the short-term usage of public cloud and private cloud, the private cloud is more expensive with a moderately high overall cost of ownership. Completely private clouds managed in-house require a large initial investment before bringing value to the company. The hardware needed to operate a private cloud is costly and will need a proficient cloud architect to manage, maintain, and set up the environment. Externally managed private clouds, though, can lessen these costs considerably.

•There might be restricted access to the private cloud for mobile users due to the high security procedures in place.

•The framework may not provide great scalability to meet unforeseeable requirements if the datacenter is restricted to in-house computing solutions. It may take additional money and time to upgrade the private cloud's obtainable resources, if there is a requirement for extra computing resources from the private cloud. Normally, this process will be lengthier than requesting extra resources from a public cloud vendor or scaling a virtual machine.

•Private cloud technologies like user self-service and increased automation can introduce some complexity into a company. These technologies usually need an IT team to redesign some of its datacenter frameworks and implement additional management tools. Accordingly, a company might have to reshape or even expand its IT staff to effectively administer a private cloud. This is not the same as the public cloud, where the cloud vendor manages majority of the underlying complexity.

•The company is solely responsible for optimizing capacity utilization in the private cloud model. An underused cloud deployment can cost the company considerably.

Private cloud service providers

Companies that have an interest in adopting private cloud, but have no access to the funds needed to invest in an in-house infrastructure, can profit from utilizing the services of a private cloud service vendor. Some of the popular providers include:

•Microsoft's Azure Stack conveys the capabilities of an advanced cloud to any company's datacenter. Azure Stack is equipped for hybridization, signifying that companies can completely utilize compliance offerings while profiting from the entire Azure cloud services when necessary.

•Hewlett Packard Enterprise is one of the strong players in the hybrid and private cloud computing industry for a long time. They provide strong services with assistance for any business requirement. Users can select the network configurations and hardware required to improve computing and storage needs. Some of their services include Managed Virtual Private Cloud, Helion Managed Private Cloud, Helion CloudSystem hardware, and Helion Cloud Suite software.

•Cisco provides on-request solutions, innovative application performance management and automated container management. Cisco infrastructure offer data security that is in harmony with workloads to improve compliance.

•VMware enables virtualization with its vSphere solution, and for private clouds, Cloud Foundation Software-Defined Data Center (SDDC).

•Dell EMC provides cloud security and management software, as well as private cloud solutions.

•IBM provides cloud orchestration and management tools, cloud security tools, IBM Managed Cloud solutions, together with private cloud hardware.

•Red Hat offers private cloud management deployment through a variety of platforms like Red Hat Cloud Suite for development and management, Gluster Storage, and OpenStack.

•Oracle's Cloud Platform.

•Hybrid cloud

This form of cloud is utilized for either Business-to-Consumer (B2C) or Business-to-Business (B2B). A hybrid cloud utilizes a private cloud core merged with the strategic use and integration of public cloud solutions. Private cloud cannot be truly isolated from the public cloud and the rest of an organization's IT solutions. Several organizations with in-house private clouds will evolve to administer workloads across public clouds, private clouds, and datacenters, thus creating hybrid clouds. By enabling the movement of applications and data and applications between public and private clouds, a hybrid cloud provides a company with more deployment choices, greater flexibility, and assist in improving existing compliance, security, and infrastructure. Companies can implement sensitive applications or mission-critical workloads on the private cloud and utilize the public cloud to manage spikes in demand or workload bursts. The objective of a hybrid cloud is to build a scalable, automated and unified environment that benefit from everything that a public cloud framework can offer, while retaining power over mission-critical data. Some of main reasons for selecting hybrid cloud include the need to avoid additional costs of hardware during expansion of existing datacenter, and for disaster recovery planning.

Hybrid cloud architecture

Constructing a hybrid cloud involves:

•A private cloud that is either built by the company in-house or acquired through a third-party private cloud vendor like OpenStack.

•A public IaaS platform like Google Cloud, Red Hat Certified Cloud, Amazon Web Services, or Microsoft Azure.

•An appropriate wide area network (WAN) or a virtual private network (VPN) connecting both environments. Many of the popular cloud vendors offers users a preconfigured VPN that is bundled together with their subscription packages. If the company decides to utilize preconfigured VPNs, they would need to insulate applications, services and users from vendor-related proprietary technologies and tools or API calls. Putting an agnostic container framework between public cloud resources and services, and users (or the organizational border) increases the capability to transfer from one cloud vendor to a different one during future migrations. Examples of available preconfigured VPNs include OpenStack Public Cloud Passport provided by OpenStack, ExpressRoute offered by Microsoft Azure, Direct Connect offered by Amazon Web Services, and Dedicated Interconnect by Google Cloud.

Hybrid cloud characteristics

The main characteristics of hybrid clouds are:

•Enables companies to keep sensitive data and critical application inside a private cloud or traditional datacenter infrastructure.

•Allows companies to capitalize on public cloud resources like IaaS for elastic virtual solutions and SaaS for the newest applications.

•Expedites portability of services, applications, and data as well as additional options for deployment models.

Use cases for hybrid clouds

The hybrid cloud is an appropriate option for the following:

•Companies serving many verticals that have different performance, regulatory, and IT security requirements. Regulations exist in certain industries in order to safeguard private data. However, not all data may be required to live in a private cloud. Hybrid cloud enables companies to act in accordance with regulations while still taking advantage of expanded computational power. After the European Union introduced the General Data Protection Regulation (GDPR), several companies have distributed their data among many solutions to fulfill the EU regulations while functioning under a separate group of regulations in the United States and other countries. Any company that manages user data globally must conform to these regulations or face severe financial penalties.

•Improving cloud investments without undermining the value proposition of either private or public cloud models.

•Enhancing security on current cloud frameworks, like SaaS services that must be distributed through secure private networks.

•Tactically undertaking cloud investments, in order to continually tradeoff and switch between the best cloud models obtainable in the market.

•Highly changeable or dynamic workloads. The future is not predictable. A software might run proficiently in its present environment today but may need extra computing power the next day. A hybrid cloud adjusts to workload requirements, letting service to operate as usual even when workload needs spike. This is known as "cloud bursting," since the workload transfers from one environment into a different environment. For instance, a transactional order entry application that gets substantial demand spikes during holiday period is a possible hybrid cloud candidate. The software could operate in private cloud, but utilize cloud bursting to request for new computing solutions from a public cloud to meet the additional demands.

•Big data processing. For instance, a company could utilize hybrid cloud storage to keep its stored test, sales, business and other data, and thereafter set up analytical queries to run in the public cloud, by scaling Hadoop or other related analytics systems to assist demanding distributed computing tasks.

•Companies needing a wider range of computing resources. For instance, a business might utilize the archival or database solutions of a public cloud vendor, but run mission-critical tasks in a private cloud.

•Introducing a new software with an untested workload brings with it a level of caution. Companies that operate in the cloud have to deal with some risks whenever they try a new approach. Hybrid cloud diminishes that risk by minimizing the need for a large initial investment. The company can deploy the latest application and only make payment for the resources it utilizes, instead of upfront payment. If the application gets shelved or fails for whatever reason, the company won't have lost a lot of money.

Benefits of hybrid cloud

The essential benefits of hybrid clouds include:

•Adaptable policy-driven deployment to allocate workloads across private and public framework based on cost, performance and security requirements.

•Public cloud resources are scaled without exposing important business workloads to the basic security threats.

•High dependability as the services are transferred across several datacenters.

•Better security standing as important business workloads run on dedicated frameworks in private clouds while non-sensitive workloads are distributed to public cloud framework to tradeoff for cost investments.

•Better control over data. Fundamentally, the hybrid model offers companies multiple choices so that stakeholders can select a framework that best suits each distinct use case.

•Cost savings depending on scale and configuration. Due to the scalability of the hybrid cloud, applications can be deployed, modified and redeployed as needed. That is ideal for peak periods during the course of the year, when it is less expensive to make payment for extra cloud services in the short term than making an investment in a private cloud infrastructure that may not be used in off-peak times.

Hybrid cloud limitations

Although hybrid cloud has some benefits, there are situations where it may not work. The downsides to hybrid cloud may include:

•It can get costly. While costs can be encouraging in some instances, they can become prohibitive in others. It is not cheap to create dedicated private servers. A public cloud model may be more appropriate for smaller companies, especially when weighed against the initial investment costs of creating and maintaining private servers.

•Privacy and security worries. Hybrid clouds raise security by allowing the company select where data and workloads are stored or performed. They also enable the capability for a company's private cloud to stay behind a firewall and then allow scaling up to a public cloud as required, restricting data exposure. On that basis, hybrid clouds can form a bigger attack surface and data passing through cloud networks can be vulnerable to similar security threats as public clouds.

•Hybrid clouds may be a poor choice for software that are latency sensitive. Information transported back and forth between the public and private sections of a hybrid cloud can produce indefensible latency.

•There is complexity involved in building an effective hybrid cloud. Without an appropriate method to connect the two cloud environments, the company is simply managing multiple clouds, and that brings about a less efficient multi-cloud approach, instead of a true hybrid cloud. Private cloud workloads have to gain entrance to and work together with public cloud, therefore, hybrid cloud necessitates solid network connectivity and API compatibility.

•For the public cloud aspect of a hybrid cloud model, there are possible service-level agreements (SLAs) infractions, connectivity issues, and other potential service disruptions. To diminish these risks, companies can design hybrid cloud workloads that can interact with several public cloud vendors. Nonetheless, this can still complicate workload testing and design. In some situations, a company would need to redesign workloads scheduled for hybrid cloud to undertake certain public cloud vendors' APIs.

•Developing and maintaining the private cloud aspect of a hybrid cloud model, would require great expertise from local cloud architects and IT staff. The execution of additional software, like helpdesk systems, databases etc., can further make a private cloud complicated. Besides, the company is entirely responsible for maintaining the private cloud, and must accommodate any modifications to public cloud service and APIs over time.

•Multicloud

This is a strategy where a company leverages more than one cloud computing frameworks to perform several tasks. Companies that want to avoid dependence on a single cloud vendor may decide to utilize resources from several vendors to get the best advantages from each distinct service. A multi-cloud framework may refer to the unification of IaaS, PaaS, and SaaS solution. It may also denote to the utilization of several public and private cloud models. A multi-cloud framework could be all-public, all-private or a mix of both. Companies utilize multi-cloud solutions to allocate computing resources, reduce the risk of data loss and downtime, and increase the available storage and computing power.

Hybrid Cloud vs Multicloud

There's a huge difference between multicloud and hybrid cloud. Multicloud has to do with the existence of more than one cloud services of the same type (private or public), obtained from different providers. Hybrid cloud involves the existence of multiple deployment models (private or public) with some form of orchestration or integration between them. A multicloud strategy could consist of two private cloud frameworks or two public cloud frameworks. A hybrid cloud strategy could consist of a private cloud framework and a public cloud framework with infrastructure (facilitated by containers, middleware, or application programming interfaces) enabling workload portability. These cloud strategies are mutually exclusive: Both cannot exist at the same time because there is either an interconnection (hybrid cloud), or there's not (multicloud). Having several cloud models, both private and public, is becoming more standard across companies as they try to improve performance and security through a diversified portfolio of environments.

Importance of containers for multicloud

One of the obstacles of a multicloud strategy is that different cloud services operate in different software frameworks. Companies want to develop software that can simply move across a wide variety of these frameworks without causing integration difficulties. Containers are the best solution because they isolate and package applications from the underlying runtime environment. This enables developers to create software that will run practically anywhere, and also facilitates the company to select public cloud vendors, based on universal standards (for example, cost, space, storage, uptime) rather than on its capability to support the company's workload caused by proprietary limitations. This portability is enabled by microservices, an architectural methodology to creating software where applications are divided into their smallest modules, separate from one another. Microservice-based applications are placed in containers. Most companies are mostly utilizing open source resources to deploy and manage these containerized applications. Kubernetes is an example of a container that has risen as the dominant system for container orchestration.

Reasons to adopt multicloud

A multi-cloud strategy enables organizations to choose different cloud solutions from different vendors because some are more appropriate for specific tasks than others are. For instance, some cloud solutions have incorporated machine-learning capabilities or focus on large data transfers. Companies adopt a multi-cloud strategy for the following reasons:

• Vendor lock-in

One of the most commonly cited reasons for adopting multicloud is the requirement to prevent becoming locked into a specific cloud provider's pricing model, add-on services, and infrastructure. Cloud-native applications dependent on microservices and containers can certainly be created to be transferrable between clouds, but vendors will usually try to make their frameworks tenacious with certain services and functions that distinguishes them from their competitors. Consequently, a portable application may not utilize a cloud vendor's full potential, leading companies to have to ascertain the trade-off between full functionality and portability -- with possible lock-in -- for specific workloads. The outcome across numerous workloads is possible to be a multicloud strategy.

• Shadow IT

A company may wind up with a multicloud approach accidentally, through the agency of shadow IT. Shadow IT is technology utilized by groups or individuals within a company that is not regulated by the company's IT department. This issue tends to come up when the company's requirements are not fully met by policy-compliant IT. Software or hardware deployed separately from the main IT team may get large enough to need more supervision. Thereupon, migrating the data and infrastructure to a preferred model (for example, public cloud) might no longer be possible. That shadow IT deployment becomes integrated into the company's current clouds, thus creating a multicloud.

•Performance

Companies can reduce latency as well as other performance metrics, like packet loss and jitter, by selecting a cloud vendor with datacenters that are physically close to their clients, since performance is usually inversely associated with the amount of network hops amongst servers. For companies that have a broad range of workloads in the cloud, the ideal solution is probably to use multiple cloud providers.

•Compliance

Several multicloud infrastructures can help companies achieve their goals for compliance regulations, risk management, and governance. Data governance requirements -- for example, the EU's GDPR -- will sometimes make sure that customer data is stored in specified locations. Unless companies intend to build and maintain their own on-site data lakes, a multicloud approach might be required, depending on a company's workload mix and geographical distribution.

•Resilience

Every cloud provider – including large ones with several geographically distributed, redundant datacenters -- undergo outages intermittently, so using only one provider may lead to the unavailability of mission-critical application. A multicloud approach may bring management and deployment concerns, but it may also bring about better resilience, disaster recovery, failover, and security. Cloud solutions like Google Cloud Platform, Microsoft Azure, and AWS deliver information on outages, but the differences in reporting make comparisons tricky. It is necessary to carry out proper research to comprehend the historical and geographical performance of the cloud solution been considered.

Multicloud automation and management

Information Technology is getting more dynamic due to virtual infrastructure both on-site and off-site. This presents significant complexity around capacity planning, financial controls, resource management, compliance and governance, and self-service. Cloud automation and management tools assists in maintaining greater oversight and visibility across these different resources. Automation has been utilized discretely within companies, with disparate tools utilized by different teams for different management domains. Nevertheless, existing automation technologies have the capability to automate assets across environments. Inserting modern automation proficiency to multicloud environments restricts the environment's complexity while improving workload performance and security for cloud-native and traditional applications.

Benefits of multicloud strategy

A multi-cloud offers options to a company. With more choices comes the capacity to capitalize on digital modification without getting locked into one service or raising a substantial initial capital. The essential benefits of multicloud include:

•Enhanced disaster preparedness

The possibility of concurrent downtime across several cloud providers is extremely low. Cloud service vendors like Amazon Web Services, Microsoft Azure, and Google Cloud Platform have remarkable service level agreements that safeguards their customers against downtime. By making use of more than two of these solutions, risk of disaster declines significantly.

•Dependable architecture

Making use of more than one cloud services creates redundancies that minimizes the risk of a single point of failure. Multicloud diminishes the possibility that downtime in one service will take the whole company offline. Adding hybridization inserts an additional level of security by storing sensitive data inside a secure, local network.

•Freedom of choice

A single cloud vendor may not be capable of providing a company with every computing services it requires. Several financial stakeholders may also be cautious of provider lock-in. If the company finds a better offer with a different provider, it may become challenging to pull away from an infrastructure that is originally designed for a different provider's cloud environment.

•Improved security

Just like hybrid cloud, multicloud empowers companies by maintaining strong security compliance while enhancing computing resources. It also minimizes the risk of downtime in mission-critical applications due to a dispersed denial of service (DDoS) attack. When even one hour of interruption can cost a company a lot financially, advanced security practices pay for themselves.

•Optimized return on investment

A multi-cloud approach enables stakeholders to select the specific services that operate best for their company. As different business requirements arise, modify and become more complicated, the company can allocate resources for particular uses, take full advantage of those resources and only pay for what is actually used.

•Lower latency

Organizations should choose cloud zones and regions that are geographically closer to their customers to reduce latency and enhance user experience. The lesser the distance for data to travel, the quicker the application will respond. All providers have cloud regions all over the world, but a single vendor may have a datacenter nearer to the customers. Utilizing a combination of several cloud providers to achieve quicker speed may be beneficial to improve applications' user experience.

•Negotiating strength

Competition holds a lot of power. A bigger company with high spend and usage may have a higher negotiating power if more than two cloud providers are pitted against each other for its business. They can leverage the diverse pricing options between providers to select the service that gives them the best value.

•Innovation

Multicloud strategy gives the flexibility to innovate quickly while getting the most out of the best-in-class or unique groups of services every cloud vendor offers. This allows developers to concentrate on innovation without compromising to meet the restrictions of one cloud vendor over another. Different from the legacy organizational method where the provider dictated the infrastructure of the enterprise applications via the features. While all cloud vendors compete to provide the best toolsets and services for everything an organization need to achieve, a multicloud strategy allows the company to choose the services and provider that best fit their needs. For example, AWS may be the best solution for video encoding, but Google Cloud may be the only cloud for annotation videos and making them searchable. Each cloud vendor has its weaknesses and strengths. Depending on the components needed to incorporate into an application, a company can select the best solutions from each vendor to build the application.

# Chapter 4: Virtualization and Cloud Computing

Virtualization is the main facilitating technology for Cloud Computing. Virtualization is technology that enables users to create numerous dedicated resources or simulated environments from a single, physical system. Software known as a hypervisor links straight to that hardware and enables users to split one system into separate, unique, and secure environments called virtual machines. These virtual machines depend on the hypervisor's capability to separate the system's resources out of the hardware and allocate them appropriately.

With the assistance of Virtualization, multiple applications and operating systems can run on similar Machine and its equivalent hardware simultaneously, increasing the flexibility and use of hardware. To put it simply, one of the key cost saving, hardware reducing, energy efficient strategy used by cloud vendors is virtualization. Virtualization allows sharing of a single physical representation of an application or a resource among multiple businesses and customers on one occasion. It does this by giving a rational name to a physical resource and offering a pointer to that resource on-demand. The word virtualization is often identical with hardware virtualization, which portrays a fundamental role in competently delivering Infrastructure-as-a-Service (IaaS) resources for cloud computing. Besides, virtualization technologies deliver a virtual framework for not only implementing applications but also for networking, memory, and storage.

Benefits of virtualization

•Increases cost savings with decreased hardware expenditure.

•Provides for easier disaster recovery and backup.

•Provides capability to manage resources effectively.

•Decreased risk of data loss, since data is backed up on several storage locations.

•Increased employee productivity due to better accessibility.

•Removal of special utility and hardware requirements.

•Smaller footprint due to lower workforce, energy and hardware requirements.

•Maximization of server capabilities, thus reducing operation and maintenance costs.

•Enables running several operating systems.

Downsides of virtualization

•Necessity to train IT employees in virtualization.

•Software licensing costs.

Types of virtualization

Virtualization can take various forms based on the type of hardware utilization and application use. Below are the main types:

•Server/hardware virtualization

This operates on the notion that an individual independent piece of a physical server or hardware, may be composed of multiple smaller hardware pieces or servers, basically consolidating many physical servers into logical servers that operate on a single principal physical server. Each little server can host a logical machine, but the whole cluster of servers is regarded as one device by all processes requesting the hardware. The hypervisor distributes the hardware resource. The main advantages include improved processing power due to application uptime and maximized hardware utilization.

Server/Hardware virtualization is further sectioned into the subsequent types:

•Paravirtualization – there is no simulation of the hardware, and the guest software operate their own isolated domains.

•Emulation virtualization – Here, unmodified software operates in modified operating system as a separate system.

•Full virtualization – Here, the entire simulation of the physical hardware occurs, to allow software to operate an unmodified guest operating system.

•Software virtualization

It offers the ability to the core computer to run and build one or more virtual frameworks. It produces a computer system equipped with hardware that allows the guest OS to run.

Software virtualization is further sectioned into the subsequent types:

•Service virtualization – hosts specific services and processes associated to a particular application.

•Application virtualization – hosts separate applications in a virtual framework different from the native operating system.

•Operating system virtualization – hosts several operating systems on the native operating system.

•Memory virtualization

It presents a way to disconnect memory from the server in order to provide a networked, distributed or shared function. It improves performance by offering greater memory size without any modification to the core memory. That is why a part of the disk drive functions as an extension of core computing memory.

Memory virtualization is further sectioned into the subsequent types:

•Operating system level consolidation – An operating system provides access to the memory pool.

•Application-level consolidation – Applications operating on connected computers directly access the memory pool via the file system or an API.

•Storage virtualization

Several network storage resources are introduced as one storage device to make it easier and more efficient to manage these resources. This provides numerous advantages like automated management, improved storage use, reduced downtime, easy updates and better availability, and enhanced storage management in a diverse IT environment.

Storage virtualization is further sectioned into the subsequent types:

•File virtualization - Storage system allows entry to files that are deposited over multiple hosts.

•Block virtualization - Numerous storage devices are merged into one.

•Network virtualization

It refers to the monitoring and management of a network as one managerial entity from one software-based administrator's console.

The purpose is to facilitate network optimization of security, flexibility, reliability, scalability, and data transfer rates. It also automates various network administrative functions. Network virtualization is especially useful for networks that encounter a huge, fast, and irregular traffic increase. The intended outcome of network virtualization provides better network efficiency and productivity.

Network virtualization is further sectioned into the subsequent categories:

•External: Combine numerous networks, or segments of networks into a simulated unit.

•Internal: Provide network like capabilities to a single system.

•Desktop virtualization

This is possibly the most common type of virtualization for any proper IT staff. The user's desktop is saved on a remote server, letting the user access the virtual desktop from any location or device. Staffs can conveniently work from home.

•Data virtualization

It allows easily manipulation of data. The data is introduced as an abstract layer fully independent of database systems and data structure. This reduces data formatting and input errors.

# Chapter 5: Cloud Computing vs Grid Computing

Grid computing is an infrastructure that connects computing resources like storage, workstations, servers and PCs and delivers the mechanism needed to access them. It is a middleware to manage different IT resources over a network, enabling them to operate as one. It is mostly utilized in universities for educational reasons and in scientific research. Grid computing and cloud computing is often mixed up, although their operations are almost alike, their operational strategies are different. Table below explains this more clearly.

Cloud Computing Grid Computing

Cloud-based applications are business specific applications like web-based application for handheld devices or thin clients Focus on research-based application with the aid of distributed independent administrative components working together to resolve a larger computing issue

Client-server architecture Distributed computing architecture

Centralized management Decentralized management system where diverse sites are spread around the world, and every site has independent administrations

Pay-as-you-go model No defined business model

Cloud services are scalable, real-time and highly flexible Scheduled services with minimal flexibility

Cloud doesn't have provision for interoperability and can cause vendor lock-in Easily deals with interoperability

Resources can be utilized in a centralized or very rarely in a decentralized way Resources are utilized in a decentralized way

Huge pool of resources Limited resources

## Chapter 6: Cloud Computing Adoption

While migrating to the cloud is a good step, it is important to proceed with caution. Irrespective of whether the company is looking at a single workload, numerous workloads, or a whole portfolio, converting from on-site to cloud-based IT necessitates more than just comprehending the technology. Effective cloud adoption requires accurate focus and a thorough blueprint, as a single mistake can become time consuming and expensive. Following a formal strategy to executing a cloud solution, reduces risk, accelerates time-to-value, and streamlines the transformation.

•Learn from other companies

Nowadays, there is an increasing number of companies migrating to the cloud. Even though each company's requirements may vary, there is still some useful lessons to learn from them. Carry out extensive research of other companies with similar capacity and size, to find out what they did to improve their IT department, their process of cloud adoption, mistakes made, and lessons learned.

•Evaluate the cloud services and providers

IT decision makers and executives must assess the challenges and opportunities of adopting a cloud computing approach in their marketplace. Once companies have concluded their research, they must develop their specific cloud approach. IT leaders should choose services and platforms that are quick to market and widely known to their industry. Decision should also be made between multicloud, hybrid, private or public cloud. When assessing provider options, focus should not be only on pricing, take other factors like continuous support, scalability and reliability into account.

•Legacy application remediation

Current applications will have to be restructured at the application and infrastructure layers to adapt to the capacity and security requirements of the cloud. These applications should be integrated with security and operate in a more automated manner. This requires significant consideration from application teams. Companies can address this challenge by creating a distinct business case for modernization of legacy applications, aligning the migration plan with major application replacements or upgrades, and implementing foundational solutions (like API frameworks) for easier remediation.

•Cultivate the appropriate skills

Professionals should be able to build cloud-based applications rapidly and securely. To accomplish this, organizations will need to employ and train cloud specialists, upskill or retrain the current employees, and establish digital-innovation labs as required with focus on cloud development.

•Security

Companies should take care to confirm that application programming interfaces and software user interfaces are secure and updated. Consistent monitoring and management of reputable tools will assist in protecting against unforeseen and malicious errors and breaches. Program bugs enables hackers to steal data or take control of cloud infrastructures. Monitoring system updates and quickly detecting vulnerabilities can help remove this risk. Inadequate due diligence in implementing cloud technologies, accidental deletion, and natural disasters can lead to malicious attacks and data loss. Companies of all sizes must create employee training programs and a cloud computing roadmap to mitigate these issues.

# Chapter 7: What is Cloud computing

Cloud computing in the simplest term means to store and access data and programs on the internet rather than on your personal hard drive.

The cloud refers to different types of software and hardware that are used collectively to make different aspects of computing available to final users as an online service.

"Cloud" in this context refers to two basic concepts which are:

Abstraction: Cloud is based widely on a virtual system therefore making applications run on unspecified physical systems with data stored in unknown locations, administrative systems outsourced to others and an omnipresent access by users.

Virtualization: Cloud computing acts as a virtual computing system that collects and shares resources whose costs are charged on a metered based basis, therefore giving room for multi-tenancy and scalable resources.

Clouds come in multiple forms. The services in which they provide may or may not be rendered by Cloud service provider. For clarity purposes, here are three examples of Cloud utilizing companies:

Google: A great amount of data centres have been created in the last decade by this prestigious company worldwide. This has enabled Google to control a great deal of advertising revenue generated worldwide which has in turn made possible the free gifting of software to clients given that the Cloud infrastructure has changed the market for user-facing software.

Amazon Web Services: this company offers users her service by letting users rent virtual computers on infrastructures owned by Amazon. It is known to be one of the most successful Cloud based enterprise.

Azure Platform: By Contrast, The Azure platform which is created by Microsoft is built for the enablement of the running of .NET Framework. This platform allows users to build and host solutions using products from Microsoft and from their data centres. It is an all-inclusive collection of cloud products that give users access to create enterprise-class without the need to build a personal infrastructure.

The above stated companies are truly revolutionary given that they enable applications to be executed with the littlest of costs and to be rapidly scaled whilst being available on-demand worldwide.

Models of Cloud Computing

Cloud computing are most commonly separated into two classes which are the most widely accepted sets of Cloud computing. As we had already stated, these classes are the Deployment models and the Service Models. Outside these two mentioned above, we have more models of Cloud computing which I shall breakdown and show you what they do. These models include:

The NIST Model:

The NIST (which is an abbreviation for National Institute of Standards and Technology) located in the U.S is a major user of Cloud computing networks given that the United States is known as one of the biggest countries in consumption of computer and tech services on a large scale.

Originally, the NIST model didn't have need for resource pooling via virtualization of a Cloud, neither was there support of multi-tenancy by a Cloud in the initial definition of Cloud computing. With Cloud computing moving towards a set of interacting components with the Service Oriented Architecture as a good example of the component. Although the NIST Cloud model doesn't take into consideration a good number of services such as transaction or service brokering, interoperability, provisioning and Integration services which are the base topic for Cloud discussion, it is easily expected that future versions of NIST Cloud model may add these features as well. The up rise in the roles of brokers, Cloud APIs and service buses at different levels, come the increasing need for these elements to be added.

The Cloud Cube Model:

This model which was designed by Jericho Forum is basically made to aid in the choosing of Cloud formations for collaborative security. Intriguingly, IT managers and Business leaders gain access to Cloud computing thanks to this Cloud model.

The Cloud Cube model takes the different "Cloud formations" in view therefore amounting to Cloud deployment and service models. Majority of Cloud providers acknowledge the importance of Cloud security to its consumers, regardless, it is a given that the Cloud customer is responsible for the accountability of the selection of desired Cloud formation to meet their personal regulatory and data location requirements. The higher in hierarchy of a Cloud service model they choose, the more the dependence on the Cloud provider to provide security and data portability ease.

In order to ensure data protection, you first of all need to systematize your data so as to know what rules are applicable to protect it, that way you ensure that you check for data sensitivity and regulatory/compliance restrictions. Once you have the above covered, you're now ready to decide what data and processes need be moved to the Cloud and which needs to be withheld and what levels you want to operate the Cloud given that Cloud models segregate into layers of business service from each other, e.g. Infrastructure/ Platform/ Software/ Process.

The Cloud cube model has 4 dimensions to which the Cloud formations are being differentiated. These are:

a) External/Internal dimension: This explains the physical location of data; it lets one know if data you try to access is inside or outside your organization's boundaries. For instance, the use of private Cloud deployment by a data centre is considered as internal while that which resides on Amazon EC2 would be considered external.

b) The Proprietary/Open dimension: This refers to the ownership condition/state of Cloud technology, services and interfaces. Through this, the degree of interoperability as well as the enabling of data transportability between your systems or other Cloud forms is well indicated and you'd be able to move data without constraint.

c) The Perimeterised/ De- Perimeterised dimension: This is basically the architectural mindset. Perimeterised refers to operation continuity within the traditional IT perimeter, signalled often by 'Network firewalls. When working in the area that is perimeterised, you can easily extend the perimeter of your organization into the external Cloud computing domain by operating the virtual server in your own IP domain using a VPN whilst using your own directory services to control access.

De- perimeterised on the other hand makes an assumption that the system perimeter is architected in accordance to the principles of the Jericho Forum's Commandments and Collaboration Oriented Architecture Framework. Data is compressed with meta-data in a de-perimeterised frame; thus, the data is protected with the mechanism to prevent it from inappropriate usage. The Cloud cube model areas which are de-perimeterised implement both internal and external domains, but sharing or collaboration of data is rather controlled by parties that organization selects to use (and are limited to these) and not defined as merely internal or external. For example if an organization feels uncomfortable about sharing certain data into the internal COA-compliant domain of a collaborating organization, they will be confident that these data will be appropriately protected using a system of encryption and key management technology to provide data confidentiality and integrity, which would also provide legal safe-harbour when the information is lost or stolen.

d) Insourced/Outsourced dimension: this describes how the delivery of cloud services you consume is being managed. It is basically a "who runs your Cloud?" situation. If the service is provided for by you or your own staff, then the service is insourced meanwhile if the provision comes from a third-party it is said to be outsourced.

There are three key questions every client should ask their cloud suppliers as suggested by the Jericho forum. This would help assure the clients on the security and protection of their data. These are:

•What is the assurance that my data stored in the Cloud services will still be available regardless of whether or not the provider changes in business direction or folds up?

•Which of the cube model is the supplier operating from in providing the cloud computing service?

# Chapter 8: Cloud Computing Deployment Models and Types

As earlier stated, a Deployment model is that which defines a Cloud's purpose and the nature of its location.

The deployment models as defined by NIST are:

The Private Cloud:

This model serves mostly companies as this type of cloud computing services is inaccessible by the public. It might exist on or off the organization's physical locations but can only be operated solely the same company. Currently known as the most secure Cloud, the private cloud processes data controlled and managed exclusively for the company without any limitation of network bandwidth, disclosure of security, and any other requirements. In the private cloud, the fundamental Cloud infrastructure could be possibly owned, operated and even managed by the company itself and/or a third-party. It gives room to too many outcomes aiding a public cloud computing environment, for example, becoming a service-based also elastic. Examples Amazon Virtual Private Cloud.

Private clouds are classified into two (2) variations which are:

The On-Premise Private Cloud

This type of private Cloud, also known as the internal Cloud, uniformly offers additional procedure plus security, but frequently runs into restrictions in terms of size and scalability. Plus, an organization's Information Technology (IT) unit would be laboured with the capital and operational costs for the physical resources with this model. Applications which facilitate total control and configurability of the different infrastructures and security are those this type of private cloud is best utilized for.

The Externally-Hosted Private Cloud

The externally-hosted private Cloud is a type of private Cloud model with its Cloud computing provider being held on the outside. This Cloud computing service provider allows for a restriction-based environment with absolute confidentiality guarantee. For organizations that don't make use of public Cloud infrastructure this type of Cloud is easily suggested to them due to the risks affiliated with the physical sharing of resources.

Some characteristics of this private Cloud include:

•Resource Dedication: with this type of Cloud, data is easily set aside and dedicated to owning enterprises.

•Enhancement in security measures: obviously we know that security is the biggest issue and client concern in the data sharing field. This Cloud model is well designed and equipped with a vast amount of state-of-the-art security and confidentiality tools poised to guarantee absolute safety.

•Better customization: adaptability and customizable user interface is a key factor that makes this cloud computing model preferred by organizations and enterprises. Businesses are able to control and keep track of their data while maintaining data security at same time.

The Public Cloud:

These are owned and managed by companies that offer quick access to cheap computing resources over a public network. Users of public cloud services are not required to purchase software, hardware or any other supporting infrastructure as this is owned by the service providers.

This Cloud model is based on a pay-as-you-go basis, therefore making it one of the easiest to setup as users aren't burdened with the task of setting up equipment. With this model, organizations only have to pay for the services they use alone. It requires no hardware device setup therefore saving the user time and money that can be invested into productivity rather than worry and management of hardware.

This cloud type is famous for its easiness in availability to the general public or a bigger institution. Regardless of its nature, clients' data are not exposed to public view.

Characteristics of this type of Cloud are:

Metered payment: because most businesses are looking for ways to cut cost while maximizing productivity, this model helps companies to achieve this as charges are only on utilized services.

Reliability and availability: ability to remain agile while being easily accessible is a desirable Cloud computing characteristic which is part of what makes this Cloud model-type widely sort after. With this, clients choose their time of convenience (which can be anytime and any day of the week) and are charged for only the times they use the services offered.

Environmental Flexibility and Elasticity: public Cloud services such as Google app engine and Amazon elastic Cloud computing serves its customers immensely by utilizing an adaptable Cloud environment which puts the power of choosing what data to share and how to share in the hands of the clients.

Self-Service: Due to the pre-configuration existing on this cloud, it makes it easy for users to operate and manage without help from the service providers. Clients do not need to be dependent on the service providers or 3rd party to ensure this feature.

The Hybrid Cloud:

This cloud type combines the foundation of the private cloud and the strategic integration and use of the public cloud services. This type of Cloud can be managed internally and privately or by a third party with hosts situated inside or outside. In reality, it is difficult for a private cloud to exist away from the rest of the company's IT resources and public cloud.  Hybrid cloud is created when companies with private clouds evolve to manage their workloads across private clouds, data centers and public cloud. This would help to reduce cost of managing private cloud as cost is split amongst all the organizations and users. Regardless of the issues concerning interoperability and Cloud standardization, organizations can still have their security and costs at a reasonable level.

The characteristics of this hybrid Cloud includes:

•Optimal use/ cutting of cost: The hybrid cloud is known for helping organizations cut cost. Instead of investing in building of infrastructure to withstand irregular bursts in system usage that rarely happens, organizations can make use of the public cloud to lay off some heavy usage and only pay for when they need it.

•Consolidation of data centers: A private cloud requires resources in typical cases as opposed to giving capacity to the most sceptical situation or circumstances. Given to the above stated, the power, maintenance, service costs, cooling as well as hardware are well incorporated.

•Risk transfer: the dangers inherent in the error of underestimating workload is transferred to the Cloud seller from the service operator thanks to the proper utilization of the Hybrid Cloud. Although Organizations are personally maintaining and running their servers and private clouds, the service provider of the public Cloud on the other hand must ensure an extreme uptime for rendered services. Quite clearly, majority of the Cloud providers own the SLAs, to which an uptime of more than 99% is guaranteed consistently.

•Availability: accessibility to corporate data centres can be quite cumbersome and costly due to the redundancy and reinforcement of data as well geographical locations. Particularly, these skillsets are usually restricted in organizations where Information Technology is not the primary focus. For hybrid cloud, the public cloud tends to go up in scale size or completely take over operations in situations where the organization's data center unavailable due to some failures and some attacks of Distributed Denial of Service (DDoS).

Community Cloud:

This infrastructure, the community Cloud, is supervised then put into utilization by a good number of institutions that seek and/or have similar core businesses, projects or shareable demand infrastructures which include but are not limited to aspects like software and hardware so that the IT costs can be sufficiently reduced. Therefore, this Cloud becomes manageable by either the joined institutions or the cloud service provider. A very good example of a community Cloud is an academic Cloud.

Types of Cloud Computing Services

There are three well known and widely accepted cloud computing services and these are:

i.Software as a Service (SaaS)

ii.The Platform as a Services (PaaS)

iii.Infrastructure as a Service (IaaS)

These Cloud computing service types are designed with consideration to modern day data centers and has integrated the three service types listed above, provided to them as utilities by enabling consumers to pay for only what they use (pay-as-you-go). The clouds run on Data hardware provided by the Data centers, and these form the foundation of the Cloud. Basically, Data centers are built out of numerous servers linked with each other; and are sited in thickly clustered bands, where the risk of a natural disaster is greatly reduced.

The Software as a Service (SaaS):

Software as a Service (SaaS) is the software distribution model that allows third party providers to host applications as well as make them accessible to customers over the internet. SaaS can be linked to the On-Demand Computing and Application Service Provider (ASP) software delivery models where the cloud owners host a single software and delivers to multiple end users over the internet. SaaS incorporates both the IaaS and the PaaS model. In this model, all customers are given access to a single copy of an application which was created specially for SaaS distribution. All customers have same application source code and in events of new updates, all customers are given the access. Based on the service level agreement between the customer and the provider, a customer's data may be stored locally, in the cloud or both in the cloud and locally. An organization for example, can create its own software and integrate the software tools with SaaS using the SaaS provider APIs. We have SaaS applications for vital business technologies like sales management, email, financial management, customer relationship management (CRM), billing and collaboration as well as Human resource management (HRM). Some tope SaaS providers are Oracle, Salesforce, Microsoft, Intuit and SAP.

In summary, SaaS lets users have easy access to software applications like emails etc over the internet.

Benefits of SaaS

•The software is available on demand globally and can be accessed over the Internet via browsers.

•Although in some cases a flat fee may be charged coupled with a maintenance fee, a typical SaaS license is subscription-based or usage-based and is billed on recurrently.

•Both software and service are monitored and maintained by the provider with no regard to where the various software components are running. A code on the client's side which is executable may exist, but the maintenance of the code or its interaction with the service isn't the client's responsibility.

•Distribution, maintenance and minimal end-user system costs are generally reduced with the SaaS service applications thus making it a lot cheaper.

•SaaS applications include features like automated updates, upgrades, and patch management.

•It is known that SaaS applications sometimes have a far lower entry barrier, an ability to scale on-demand and at a recurring cost as opposed to their locally installed adversaries.

•Software version is the same for all users in order for them to be compatible with each other.

•Multiple users are supported by SaaS which provides a shared data model through a multi-tenancy model at a single-instance.

The Platform as a Service (PaaS)

Platform as a Service (PaaS) is a type of cloud computing where third party provides both software and hardware tools over the internet, this mostly applies to software for application development. The service provider hosts the software and hardware on infrastructure belonging to the host. This alone makes users free from installing software and hardware in-house to run or develop a new application.

With PaaS, a business entire IT infrastructure are not replaced rather the business gets its key services from PaaS. This include Java development or application hosting.

A PaaS provider creates and supplies a strong and improved environment for users to be able to install applications and data sets. Rather than worrying about building and managing infrastructures and services, businesses are able to focus on building and running applications.

Most products under PaaS are built towards software development. From this platform, we get storage infrastructure along with version management, text editing, compiling and text services that aids developers to create improved and better software.

A very good example of Platform as a Service (PaaS) according to the given explanation will be SQL database, Microsoft's Azure.

Systems for PaaS could be anything from developer platforms like Windows Azure Platform to systems like Drupal, Squarespace, Wolf, and others where the tools are modules that are very well developed with nearly no need for coding.

That being said, PaaS models include a good number of services, amongst which are:

•Development of Applications: PaaS creates a means for user-crafted programs to be in supported language or for a visual development environment to have the code written for you.

•Collaborative capability: many users can use PaaS systems as a means to collectively work on the same projects and/or share resources.

•Management of data: accessing and using of data in data store is made possible by using provided tools set for that purpose, and data can be stored in either the service of the PaaS provider's or a third-party storage service.

•Instrumentation, performance, and testing: for applications, tools are made available for the measuring and optimization of the user's performance.

•Transaction management: services such as transaction management or brokerage are provided for by most PaaS systems. This provides for the maintenance of transaction integrity.

As the vibrancy of PaaS third party add-ons, applications, tools, services and associated markets ascend, the better they are, and these functionalities allow you to extend your application via purchase of functionality which is in most cases cheaper than rolling your own. The tools needed to construct different types of applications are provided by the PaaS for the enablement of working together in the same environment, among which the most common application types are:

•Composite business applications

•Data portals

•Mash-ups of multiple data sources

Data sharing must be enabled in these applications to allow it run in a multi-tenant environment and help the applications work in tandem much easier which is why, a common development language such as Java or Python is usually offered.

The Infrastructure as a Service (IaaS)

Infrastructure as a Service (IaaS), is the most comprehensive of all the cloud computing models. In the IaaS, the customers are given liberty to utilize and run as many software as they need such as operating applications and systems, given that they have the backing of the suppliers who provide all the required networks storage, processing, and other necessary resources for computing. The customers have absolute power over the operating systems such as implemented application and space. Here, a computer environment or infrastructure (preferably called software and hardware) is provided for by this Cloud computing model.

In summary, Infrastructure as a Service (IaaS) is a cloud computing service model in which the cloud virtualizes hardware. In this particular model, the servers, storage, network infrastructure, and so forth are owned by the service vendor.

The payment scheme here is also defined and incurred based on usage, meaning that users only pay for services used at the rate of storage per gigabytes just like internet mobile data is calculated in gigabytes and similarly data transfer or usage computing per hour.

An example which best suits this type of Infrastructure as a Service (IaaS) based on the above statements is Firewall hosts. Another example of the IaaS is the Amazon's Web Services Elastic Compute Cloud (EC2) or Secure Storage Service (S3)

Benefits of the IaaS:

•Saves Cost: an obvious pro of using the IaaS model is the reduction in cost of infrastructure. Given that the IaaS is based on a metered system of charging customers, organizations choose to use this service model as they no longer have to worry about ensuring their system stays running, hardware maintenance, replacing of old equipment etc. The IaaS is also sort after as it requires no upfront payment, or charges for unused services.

•Flexible scalability: the IaaS is preferred in the eyes of its users due to its ability to scale up when more systems are needed and scaling down to release these virtual systems into the Cloud all in a bid to suit the user's current needs. This on-demand flexible scalability helps the IaaS respond with agility to the possibly constant change in a customer's requirements, a feature which is good for running expendable tests.

•Fast Response Time: thanks to the agility of the IaaS in responding to needs, user organizations can respond to client needs quicker than their competitors thus keeping them ahead of the curve in terms of productivity and delivery.

•Support for Disaster Recovery, Back Up and high availability: this simply means the IaaS has very versatile and prolific measures put together as a fail-safe plan in case of a disaster which would have in other cases of computing methods caused them to lose data and/or cost them so much money on recovery. This includes everything the organization needs to function as usual and at a recovery speed that turns what would have been a hole in productivity to merely a road bump.

•Focus on business growth: with all of the above stated weight and responsibilities taken off the shoulders of the users, they gain more time to focus on the business whilst saving time, money and energy which can now be invested in productivity without the unnecessary worry like- data loss, security, and cost of maintenance etc. that come with other forms of computing.

Amongst these three service models, it is easily noticeable that IaaS is the service model out of the rest that has maximum control over the infrastructure providers. When put in comparison with IaaS, PaaS has far lesser control over the infrastructure providers. Every service the IaaS offers its clients, are part and parcel of the responsibilities of the Cloud provider.

# Chapter 9: Virtualization of Service models

What is virtualization?

Virtualization simply refers to the creation of a non-physical version of a server, operating system, storage devices or network resources, with the full capabilities of the physical one but without the hardware unit. Think of it like 'Faith', you can have it, base belief on it, use it, but in actuality it isn't a physical thing you can hold irrespective of the fact that it exists.

Virtualization is a technique that allows different users, organizations and customers to share a single physical instance of an application or a resource. This is done simply by giving a logical name to the physical storage then create pointers that users, customers can use to access the physical storage when needed.

Virtualization is aimed at the management of workloads by turning traditional computing into a more scalable, efficient and economical system of computing. Think of Virtualization of technology as the reduction of hardware which helps to save cost and energy.

What is the Concept Behind Virtualization?

Hardware virtualization is creating a virtual (non-physical) machine over already existing hardware and operating system. With a virtual machine, the environment is logically separated from its underlying hardware.

The Host Machine is the machine on which the virtual machine is created on while Guest Machine refers to the virtual machine itself.

Architecture of Virtualized Technology

Virtual allocation of computing space and/ or memory is usually set aside for server users. These servers require a host (platform) on which a hypervisor (i.e. the software through which the hardware is interacted with) runs. The virtualized model is made up of users of Cloud computing, service models, virtualized models and its host software and their accompanying hardware. The virtualization software makes the running of multiple instances of operating systems and multiple applications on the same server at the same time, and is based on three stated service models which are; SAAS (software as a service), PAAS (platform as a service) and IAAS (infrastructure as a service).

•SAAS makes applications available to the cloud users as it suits their needs.

•PAAS gives the cloud users a common ground (platform) on which their applications can be executed.

•IAAS provides the Cloud's resources, the security and hardware required for their maintenance.

Two things to remember in virtualization are

Host: for virtualization purposes, the hypervisor software runs on a virtualization platform called the "Host".

Hypervisor: the software with which the virtual machine is being used to work under the virtually simulated environment is called "Hypervisor".

Comparing Traditional Servers to Virtual Servers

Basic Traditional Servers

These are usually managed by a system administrator and consist of an operating system, the hardware, the storage and the application. When this type of server becomes filled, it has to be replaced immediately.

Advantages of the Traditional Servers

a. Easy deployment

b. Back-up is easy

c. Can run applications virtually.

Disadvantages

a. Cost effectiveness of hardware maintenance.

b. Difficulty in replication.

c. Unable to update physical infrastructure.

d. Difficulty in implementation of redundancy.

Virtual Servers

Virtual servers deal with the software aspect of computing whilst doing away with the need for hardware. Virtual servers consist of an operating system, storage and an application.

Advantages of Virtual Servers

a. IT pool maintenance.

b. High availability of hardware.

c. Use of a virtually based environment.

d. Lesser heat and energy consumption as lesser hardware is used.

Types of Virtualization

Virtualization in Cloud computing can be done in fours ways as explained below:

1. Hardware Virtualization: When the Virtual machine manager (VMM) otherwise known as virtual machine software is installed directed

on the hardware system, we call this hardware virtualization.

The key work of the hypervisor is to monitor and control the memory, processor as well as other hardware resources.

Once the virtualization of hardware system is done, installation of different operating systems become possible as well as running different apps on the OS.

Uses of Hardware Virtualization

This is mostly for server platforms, because it is easier to control virtual machines than it is to control physical servers.

2. Server Virtualization: When the Virtual machine manager (VMM) otherwise known as virtual machine software is installed directly on the Server System, we call this server virtualization.

Uses of Server Virtualization

This is done due to the ability of dividing a single physical server into multiple servers based on demand and also for balancing weight load.

3. Operating System Virtualization: When the Virtual machine manager (VMM) otherwise known as virtual machine software is installed on the Host Operating system rather than the hardware system, we call this operating system virtualization.

Uses

This is used mostly to test applications on different OS platforms.

4. Storage Virtualization: has to do with the grouping of physical storage from several network storage devices to make it look like it is a single storage device. This is implemented with the aid of software applications.

Uses

This type is mostly used to back-up and also for recovery purposes.

Why Virtualization?

We should virtualize because of the following reasons:

a.Isolation: it aids isolate users from each other thus even though they share the same software, all of a user's personal data isn't exposed; thereby making open collaborations easier.

b.Resource sharing: Huge amounts of resources can be dissected into redundant virtual resources so that multiple users can use it via virtualization techniques.

c.Dynamical resources: unlike the difficulties experienced with the traditional servers when it comes to reallocation of resources, it is quite easy to reallocate resources ranging from storage, to computational resources.

d.Resource Aggregation: the small available resources, through virtualization, can be increased to a larger extent.

# Chapter 10: Characteristics, Benefits, Advantages and Disadvantages of Cloud computing

A lot of aging concepts of technology come together to form the building blocks of Cloud computing which can make it difficult for the new generation of technology savvies and/or users who are new to the whole Cloud computing concept, find it easy to understand. Cloud computing is obviously revolutionary and comes with benefiting characteristics which could enable users know the technological know-how on how to utilize it with full optimization.

Among these characteristics include:

•The Paradigm Shift in Cloud computing:

On choosing a Cloud service provider, a good portion of what is an enormous infrastructure of linked computer storages, network capacities and actively functioning data centers, would be leased to you for as long as you use and pay for it. Most of these data centers are run by large multi-million-dollar companies. There's been estimate of how much a state-of-the-art microchip facility can cost which is anywhere between 2 to 5 billion dollars (this estimate was done to aid you get a whiff of the scaling). Most large providers of Cloud computing service have multiple data centers located everywhere in the globe, and by comparison, a Cloud computing data center can be run with the cost range of 100 million dollars (this is for state-of-the-art data centers). Usually, more accurate counts of data centers are often difficult to obtain, but it's known that Google has at least 35 data centers whilst Amazon's web services Cloud has at least 20 data centers; both of which are situated worldwide.

The American military created an initiative in the 1960s whose primary focus was the reduction of electronics. This initiative saw that funds were inputted into a good number of the semiconductor lines of production, thus leading to the creation of advanced microprocessors, dense memory arrays, and the sophisticated integrated circuit technology used in making computers, and mobile devices and a lot more of present-day technological devices. A good number of large companies were forced or rather coaxed by the commercialization of the internet, to build gigantic computing infrastructures to give their businesses the required support.

The infrastructure, that is, 'Amazon.com', was built to support elasticity in demand to allow the systems accommodate traffic peaks on busy shopping days such as "Black Friday". Amazon had to open its network to partners and customers as Amazon web services due to the capacity idleness it underwent.

On the other end, Google's business has overtime experienced an exponential growth that has prompted it to set up and build a worldwide array of data centers. Built in 2006, one of Google's data center situated in Dallas, Oregon, is said to be the size of an American football field.

Whilst these data centers have in their various ways increased in size, other businesses have grown their Cloud computing data centers as "Greenfield" projects. It is noticeable that these data centers have been known to take these into consideration when setting up site:

i)Have proximity to water in abundance.

ii)Ensure that system latency is completely optimized.

iii)Situate centers where there are high-speed network backbone connections.

iv)Ensure power cost in situated area is low

v)Gain leverage of renewable power supply.

vi)Be unobtrusive in terms of keeping costs of land and occupation modest

vii)Obtain tax breaks.

If all the above stated are provided, there's little to absolutely no chance that the efficiency of a Cloud computing networks in the data centers would be flawed given that this would enable the making of utility computing profitable as it captures enough margin.

These companies are quite big energy consumers as they consume roughly about 10 percent of the world's total power. These companies like Google for instance may become major players in the 21st century production of energy. Cloud computing has become such a big deal thanks to the internet's creation of technological utilities.

Services and applications that aid productivity which are delivered online as Cloud computing applications have undergone proliferation over the last couple of years. Regardless of the fact that not a lot of people implement the once straightforward client-to-server deployment of the internet, Cloud computing still has exemplary impact which abounds in our everyday life.

In many cases, the same applications which are Cloud hosted support the on-premises deployment and the transparent movements of said applications to the Cloud.

A case study is Channeladvisor.com. Their auction listings and sales management have been known to have many users. The site recently included a CRM connector to salesforce.com after its expansion to include more services.

Thanks to Cloud computing, software delivery has experienced a major shift in the economics in a manner quite similar to that of how music streaming caused the shift in the delivery of commercial music. Cloud computing has enabled new vendors of software the ability to create productivity aiding applications at prices much lower than would be possible before now due to the advantages in Cloud computing. Given the decline in the number of bib box computer stores alongside the purchase of older and orthodox retail computer models, gaining a market to sell said system types has become increasingly difficult for them. Take Wal-Mart vendors as a case study.

Meanwhile, the much more sort after new models of computer applications allows vendors, like Google, to offer applications like complete office suites for free to people, individually; with the support of the subscription models of their advertiser. Google itself as a business has had some major successes in comparison to the industry leader, Microsoft Office. Few years ago, this partly caused the Los Angeles County' switch to Google Docs.

According to the Definition of Cloud Computing by NIST, as earlier stated, the classification of cloud computing sub-sections into three SPI service models (SaaS, IaaS, and PaaS) and four cloud types (public, private, community, and hybrid) and also assigns five essential cloud computing characteristics that systems must render:

•On-demand self-service: provisions for computer resources can be made available with no need for interaction with personnel of the Cloud service provider. Computing capabilities, which include server time and/or network storage, can unilaterally be provided for by users without supervision of the Cloud's service provider or any other human middleman's interaction.

•Broad network access:  even with the most standard of methods, resources available on the Cloud are easily accessible and enable clients of all ramifications the provision of platform-independent access. More so, the access is available to clients irrespective of device which could range from heterogeneous operating systems to devices such as laptops and mobile phones. These computing capabilities are available via the internet or networks which are easily accessible via the utilization of standard and channelled mechanism, all of which is made to encourage people to make use of heterogeneous platforms.

•Resource pooling: resources which are created by the provider of the Cloud service are pooled together in a system which supports multi-tenant usage. All of the systems, both physical and virtual, are allocated or reallocated dynamically as required. This concept of pooling is the idea of abstraction that hides the location of resources such as virtual machines, processing, memory, storage, and network bandwidth and connectivity. The provider's computing resources serve multiple users after being pooled together. Location independence is not a luxury the customers enjoy here as they have no control neither are they knowledgeable about the exact location of the services they are being provided with, although they might be able to specify the location at a higher abstraction level.

•Rapid elasticity: Resources can be provisioned for at a rate that is both rapid and elastic. These resources can be added by the systems when they either, scale up the systems thus adding more powerful computers or scaling out the systems with computers of the same kind. The demands from customers gain commensuration from the scaling of systems given that the scaling may either be automatic or manual depending on the client's standpoint. Cloud computing is a limitless resource pooling system which can be acquired via purchase at any time and any desired quantity, as is their resources.

•Measured service: The use of cloud system resources is measured, audited, and reported to the customer based on a metered system. Using a standardized metric system such as storage usage amount, transaction number, bandwidth or network I/O (Input/Output), a client can incur charges based on a good range of rate types including processing power used. Charges are incurred by the client only for the services they use. In this situation, Cloud computing systems are automatically controlled with optimization for the leveraged resources. Given the already mentioned metering capabilities which are utilized for abstraction, a lot can be done by resources example monitoring, controlling and making provision for data transparency, for the user as well as its provider as far as service implementation is concerned.

Benefits of cloud computing

It's well-known that the features/ characteristics of cloud computing listed above can as well be seen as benefits of using cloud computing but we thought it'd be of added value to you to list the following additional advantages:

•Ease of utilization: quite often, depending on the type of service you're being offered by your Cloud computing service provider, you may get to realize that you do not require hardware or software licenses to implement the services received.

•Simplification of maintenance and upgrade: patches and upgrades are much more easily applied thanks to how centralized the systems are. This means access and updates are given freely to users who seek to keep their software up to date.

•Quality of Service: under contract, the quality of service is negotiable whilst purchasing Cloud computing services from a vendor. You can ask for the service to be optimized to meet your needs.

•Reliability: the ability of Cloud computing networks to upscale or downsize, and be open to optimization to meet users' needs with no more pressure or expenditure than required whilst balancing load makes them so much more reliable, even more reliable than one can be achieved by a single organization.

•Lower Costs: it is common knowledge around these parts that Cloud computing networks and services alike are created to run at higher efficiencies and greater utilization with inversely proportional costs while being effortlessly reliable.

•Low Barrier to Entry: with Cloud computing it doesn't cost much to setup a network and get things running. Regardless of how little one starts or how little the upfront start-up capital expenditure is, with Cloud computing, one can easily expand to a big size in little to no time without the unnecessary fears that come with hardware networking.

•Outsourced IT management: in cloud computing, you can easily use the deployment model feature which outsources to third party to manage your computing infrastructure while you focus on the actual running of the business aspect with far lesser fear of security issues. In most cases, you save cost from employing IT staffs.

Disadvantages of cloud computing

The advantages are numerous, however, like many other computing systems, Cloud computing has its fair share of disadvantages.

•Even with the number of benefits of Cloud computing being multitudinous, there are just as many disadvantages as there are advantages. Generally, there's a colloquial rule that the Cloud computing advantages have to present a mire coaxing and compelling pitch for small organizations than is required when pitching to larger ones. There's usually support for IT staff and efforts for development provided for by these larger companies that create room for software solutions which are created to cater peculiar issues and particular needs.

•When a service in the Cloud or an application is being put into use by you, you are utilizing something that isn't technically as customizable as you might want it to. In addition, applications which are deployed on-premise still carry many more features in comparison to their Cloud counterparts although in many cases, these Cloud applications also have this capability.

•All Cloud computing applications have been known to suffer from inherent latency which is actually an intrinsic part of the connectivity of their Wide Area Networks. Though Cloud computing applications are known to do marvellously well when it comes to large-scale processing of tasks, Cloud computing isn't a good model suggestion if the applications you run require large amounts of data transfer.

•Also, just like the internet, Cloud computing is a stateless system because it is virtual thus information is necessarily unidirectional in nature in order for communication to be able to survive on distributed systems. The service provider receives all your requests in the forms of 'HTTP:', PUTs, GETs, and so on, to which you wait on the service provider who then sends a response using what may seem as a conversation between client and provider, but in actuality is done with a disconnect between the two. Now, this disconnect creates a gap, thus causing messages to travel over multiple routes and resulting in the data's arrival to be out of sequence. Regardless, when this happens, many other known characteristics of Cloud computing aid the communication to still succeed despite the medium's faultiness. Therefore, for transactional coherency to be imposed upon the system, transaction managers, service brokers, and other forms of middleware must be added to the system as additional overhead and this can easily lead to an introduction of a very large amount of performance hit on some applications.

•Privacy and security would undoubtedly be an area of common interest to most Cloud computing users. As your data travels over and rest on systems that are no longer within your power or authoritative control, there's a risk tendency of data getting into the wrong hands due to the occurrence of interception of others and this is why you would not be able to count on the vendor or Cloud provider to maintain your privacy especially when faced with governmental actions. Remember this is just a tendency.

Take the United States as a case study with focus on the millions of phone calls which ran from AT&T and Verizon that was extracted by the National Security Agency using a data analyser to extract security matching phone calls.

Another good example is the Chinese case with Google services, which had undergone a content removal filter that caused the government of China to step in and object.

All of this occurred because Google realized, after five years of operation that Chinese hackers were breaking into and accessing Gmail accounts of Chinese citizens and all of this ended as Google had to move their servers from Google.ch to Hong Kong.

So, whilst the Cloud computing industry continually undergoes redress to both old and new security threats and concerns, if you work with sensitive data it is advised that you be aware, particularly of the issues involved just so you can make a wiser computing services decision.

•Nowadays, more and more organizations get faced with a plethora of regulatory compliance issues. In the United States, companies must act in compliances with the Sarbanes-Oxley Act as a major part of their accounting requirements. Such requirement may take different forms for different example; health care providers have data privacy rules by the HIPAA to which they must be in compliance to. In Europe, the European Common Market has a boat-full of its own legislation that companies have to deal with too. Said rules apply to data in transit differently from as they do data at rest. Having said that, in situations where data is being run through lines that cut across multiple states and/or countries, you may suffer with having to comply with multiple jurisdiction issues. Not much support can be expected from Cloud computing system vendors in such cases where the government is involved, and this causes much of the burden sometimes the entire burden to be put on the client. In a big paraphrase, Cloud computing is a risky area to go to in terms of compliances.

Understanding Cloud Architecture

Naturally, Cloud computing is an extension of various principles of designs, protocols and systems which have developed over the course of the past 20 years. Cloud computing displays some new abilities which are designed into an application stack with responsibility for resource programmability, scalability and virtualization. The composability characteristics of Cloud computing is a term used to describe the Cloud's ability to build applications from component parts. A platform can be said to be a Cloud computing service in that it has both hardware and software, and can be used to create more complex software with virtual appliances.

# Chapter 11: Exploring the Cloud Computing Stack

Cloud computing can be broken down into two architectural layers:

•A client as a front end

•The "cloud" as a backend

The above stated descriptions are the two basic layers of what actually comprises of multiple component layers and complementary functionalities with a fine mixture of standard and proprietary protocols. In some cases, Cloud computing may be distinguished from older models using the Application Programming Interface (API) which often controls the information technology service and helps modify the delivered services on the network.

Under this, we would look at 6 ways of exploring the cloud computing stacks listed here:

•Composability

- Infrastructure

- Platforms

- Virtual Appliances

- Communication Protocols

- Applications

Composability

Cloud-built applications often have a collection of components that build a property. This feature is referred to as composability. Services which can be tailored for specific purposes using standard parts are assembled using components of a composable system. These composable component must be:

- Modular: it is an independently cooperative and self-contained unit which is reusable, and replaceable.

- Stateless: it can undergo and execute a transaction with no effect or regard to other transactions and/or requests.

Transactions are required to be stateless. A couple of Cloud computing applications can through brokers, service buses and transaction monitors, provide managed states and in more peculiar cases, full transactional systems are deployed in the Clouds although this would be hard to architect in distributed architecture. Although software and hardware composability are not necessarily a requirement in Cloud computing from the user or developer's standpoint, it is a highly sort after feature given that it makes implementation of system designs easier whilst making solutions more portable and interoperable.

Cloud computing systems have the tendency of reducing in composability for users as the incorporation of more services to the Cloud computing stack increases. For IaaS (Infrastructure as a Service) vendors such as Amazon Web Services, GoGrid, or Rackspace, there's no wisdom in offering to customers who are most certainly deploying applications on standard operating systems such as Linux,

Windows, Solaris, etc., non-standard machines.

The logic surrounding the idea that composability diminishes as you go up the Cloud computing stack is from the users' perspective because if you are a service provider of PaaS or SaaS, the responsibility of creating the platform or service to be presented to the reseller, user or developer, rests on your shoulder and this makes working with a composable system a very powerful notion.

That being said, a PaaS or SaaS service provider gets the same benefits that a user does—from a composable system. These benefits among other include:

•No difficulty in system assembling

•System development at cheaper costs

•More reliable operation

•A greater number of qualified developers

•A design methodology which is logical

The module itself can be written in any programming language that best suits the developer although this isn't always specified. From standpoint, the system module is more of a black box, in which only the interface is well specified. Thanks to this independence, the internal activities of the components and modules can be interchanged for a different model at will as long as the specifications of the interface remain the same.

Infrastructure

Providers of large Infrastructure as a Service (IaaS) are dependent on virtual machine technology for the delivery of servers for the running of applications. Described in terms of a machine image, virtual servers have been known to be described in terms of realistic servers with which a given number of microprocessor (CPU) cycles, network bandwidth and memory access can be delivered to customers. Said virtual machines serve as containment assigned specifically for resources and run the software which in turn defines the Cloud computing system utility.

Virtual servers present a new perspective in the programming of applications. For example, when software is being created, it requires several tasks to be performed in parallel, the programmer might write an application to create additional threads of execution that need be managed by the application. When a Cloud service application is created by a developer, they can have the best suited services attached to the application allowing it to scale the execution of the program.

Platforms

Platform in Cloud computing simply refers to a software layer that is used in the creation of service of a higher level. As we discussed earlier, many different Platform as a Service (PaaS) providers render services designed to give developers different capabilities. Cited here are three major PaaS examples:

•SalesForce.com's Force.com Platform

•Windows Azure Platform

•Google Apps and the Google App Engine

The difference between a platform and a virtual appliance is that the installed software is a construct of components and services controlled through an API that the platform provider publishes.

It is quite reasonable for system vendors to transfer their development environments to the Cloud with Web applications successfully created with similar technologies, therefore, NetBeans Integrated Development Environment (IDE) can be found to be included in a platform which is based on a Sun xVM hypervisor virtual machine which also supports the Sun GlassFish Web Stack and programmable using Perl or Ruby. Developers who use windows might be provided with a platform by Microsoft for them to be able to run a Hyper-VVM, use the ASP.NET framework, Support applications such as SQL (which is an enterprise application), and be Visual Studio programmable. This will allow for usable applications to be created in the Cloud for multiple users.

Often times, platforms come with a plethora of application design-aiding tools and utilities. Inclusively, one may also find developer tools for team collaboration, tools for storage, program and attribute measuring instrumentation, tools for testing, versioning, and tools for database and web service integration, all of which are dependent on the providing vendor.

Similar to how virtual appliances open themselves to users via an API, so also does a Cloud-built application which implements a platform service use the service through its own API. This will then allow for interaction between users and the platform as the service consumption is being carried out via the API thus making the scaling and management of the services to be carried out appropriately by the platform. HTML,

JavaScript, etc. are sometimes offered to users of some platforms as interface development tools. More and more developers are choosing to work with rich internet environments such as Adobe Flash, Air, Flex, or other alternatives given to how increasingly the web has become media-oriented. The platform API gets abstracted away from user interface thus making the UI have to manage said services.

Virtual Appliances

The term "Virtual appliances" may be a little misleading because it gives the mental picture of a device with a narrow purpose. Virtual appliances are software which are installed on virtual servers. A virtual appliance is a platform instance which occupies the middle of the Cloud computing stack. Web Server applications, Database server applications, and the likes can run on a virtual machine images thus referred to as virtual appliances.

A virtual appliance is a deployment object common in the Cloud and is an area with considerable amount of activity and innovation. The ability to utilize appliances as basis for complex service assembling is a major advantage of virtual appliances given that the appliance is now one of your standardized components, thus aiding your system management to be easier as the need for application configuration and maintenance is removed.

Communication Protocols

Implemented standard Internet protocols alongside the underlying transfer protocols (like HTTP and HTTPS) aid in the rise of Cloud computing through services available on the internet.

Computed and data resources in the Cloud are easily exposed using standards and protocols which come in form of either format data or communications, which are sent over these 2 protocols. For inter-process communication (IPC) processes to be carried out, networking lines have had various client/server protocols applied to them during distribution over the years. Various forms of RPC (Remote Procedure Call) implementations (including DCOM, Java RMI, and CORBA) make effort to resolve issues involving service engagement and transaction management over what is a stateless network. Web-centric RPC technology's XML-RPC is its first service in which platform-independent XML data is used in the encoding of programmed calls which are carried over the HTTP (which is the networking transport all users are linked).

Thanks to WSDL and SOAP, web services are allowed to describe additional properties and methods they could provide all of which is made possible through the created WSDL and SOAP extensions. Said extensions are known under the name of WS-*, or the "WS-star". Among which include:

•WS-Addressing

•WS-Discovery

•WS-Eventing

- WS-Federation

- WS-MakeConnection

- WS-Messaging

- WS-MetadataExchange

- WS-Notification

- WS-Policy

- WS-ResourceFramework

- WS-Security

- WS-Transfer

- WS-Trust

Now, metadata can be added to SOAP messages thanks to the above stated specifications which serves as a standard for data adding by modifying message headers while simultaneously ensuring the body structure is untouched. Furthermore, the WSDL XML message has the standard method for metadata exchange added onto it.

These WS-* services gain access to the remote server applications using the SOAP protocol which carries over XML messages, in ways which are increasingly becoming more complex as opposed to earlier methods in which gateways like CGI are provided by clients or servers to aid access media contents on the servers thus making the servers get burdened by accepting and processing very complex requests from the current data communications or conversing with their clients on sophisticated negotiations which need the minimization of processing information as responses are being exchanged.

Applications

Despite the fact that there are many details in which a Cloud computing stack encapsulates, it is not good enough in terms of expressing and giving account of all considerations required of any deployment. Omissions are noticeable in the behaviour of distributed Web applications and the Internet protocols designed to serve as a stateless service (by that we mean the internet's design to respect each request as an independent transactions).

Greater percentage of the work needed to be carried out is done by computer systems that are stateful, despite the fact that stateless servers are easier for architects to draw-up and stateless transactions more resilient to outages.

Transaction servers, message queuing servers and other middleware have been designed to bridge the issues of having really hard development efforts going into the making of Web properties useful in commerce and focused on the creation of mechanisms which change a set of stateless transactions to stateful ones. This problem, to an extent, has been known to be common in Cloud computing thus needing the implementation of a variety of constructs to solve identified issues.

## Chapter 12: Connecting to the Cloud, Cloud Storage and Migration

Cloud computing services can be accessed in a number of ways the two most common of which are:

•A Web browser

•A proprietary application

These two are most commonly used as they can run on a server, a PC, a mobile device, or a cell phone. These devices similarly utilize this type of applications, this refers to how they exchange data using an insecure and transient medium. That being said, three basic methods for securing said connections are:

•Use a secure protocol to transfer data such as SSL (HTTPS), FTPS, or IPsec, or connect using a secure shell such as SSH to connect a client to the cloud.

•Create a virtual connection using a virtual private network (VPN), or with a remote data transfer protocol such as Microsoft RDP or

Citrix ICA, where the data is protected by a tunnelling mechanism.

•Encrypt the data so that even if the data is intercepted or sniffed, the data will not be meaningful.

Clients who want the best connections rely on at least two of the above stated techniques during their communication with the Cloud. Web services are being relied upon by clients to make available secure connections but as time goes on, there is likelihood that clients themselves will ensure a secure connection without the mentioned dependence.

Take a café's network connection for instance, it is noticed that in some cases access to systems on their network aren't protected by firewall; worse still, the firewall isn't properly configured. This is the reason people prefer to carry routers with properly configured firewalls with them because these routers also come with in-built VPNs.

To that, here are three other recommended VPNs for secure connection purposes:

•Hotspot VPN (http://www.hotspotvpn.com/)

•Anchor Free Hotspot Shield (http://hotspotshield.com/)

•Gbridge (http://www.gbridge.com/)

Cloud Storage

Cloud storage as the name implies refers to the service to which where data is managed, stored, and backed up remotely. Users can access the Cloud storage using a network (usually the internet is the go-to network) and also store files online which can be retrieved from any location and time via the internet. The files are being kept on an external server and made available by the provider company. This gives provider companies ease in terms of data storage although it can be quite costly. Users need to back-up their stored data because recovering Cloud-stored data is a lot slower than recovering data from a traditional back up. Cloud storage is the lower layer of Cloud computing system which supports the service of the other layers above it.

Popular Cloud Storage Options

Listed below are a couple of Cloud-based storage services many of which provide up-to gigabytes in storage space for free, with promise for additional space at a monthly fee. These Cloud storage services, like all Cloud storage services, provide a simple drag-and-drop system of access whilst ensuring that data is synced between all of the user's devices. They also let users with signed-up accounts collaborate with each other.

DROPBOX

Collaboration: Users of Dropbox are able to upload and share entire folders with fellow Dropbox users via the Dropbox web interface, the Dropbox desktop client or other supported apps and devices. These folders can be viewed by all collaborators of the given folder. A user can either choose to store a file privately for personal purposes or publicly to enable others gain access. Files set as "Public" can be accessed by both Dropbox and non-Dropbox users. However, unlike Dropbox users, non-Drobox users must download the file to open or use it and any changes made to their copy of the folder will not reflect on that of the original Dropbox user's folder.

Mobile App Support: Devices such as phone and tablets can easily access documents using the Dropbox mobile app.

Storage: Dropbox offers 2GB of free storage.

Strengths

Its biggest strength would be its ease of use. One can simply share a document or folder by using their device's native share function. Also, Data recovery is far easier with Dropbox than with most options. You can also decide what data syncing speed you'd prefer.

Weaknesses

It offers one of the lowest amounts of free storage.

Google Drive

Collaboration: in order to access documents stored with this option, users must own an account. Every change in document by the creator or collaborator is automatically synced and reflected upon the document. You will be notified of every change in the document if you own it.

Mobile App Support: Google Drive is available on Androids with options of downloading application or accessing via web browsers. You can even share Google Drive files to your contacts.

Storage: Google Drive offers 5GB of free storage.

Strengths

Google Drive comes with a built-in editor for documents which help ease editing of documents without need for third-party apps.

It can be accessed via other Cloud based apps like ES File Explorer which aids in sharing flexibility.

Weaknesses

Sharing is quite difficult here in comparison to Dropbox— you need to have the web application to set it up. Speed of uploads and syncing are greatly influenced by your network.

Microsoft SkyDrive

Collaboration: data can be shared and accessed via Microsoft SkyDrive with or without accounts. You can also live-edit data online.

Mobile App Support: SkyDrive can be accessed using both a Window's phone app and an iOS (iPhone/iPad) app. Users are enabled to view and share as well as edit and update files via phone or tablet. Third party iOS apps, such as Pages and Keynote can access SkyDrive files.

Storage: SkyDrive offers 7GB of free space.

Strengths

It is the biggest in comparison to the others listed here in terms of space and just like Google Drive, you can edit documents within the browser, without having to use a third-party application like Microsoft Word.

Weaknesses

The interface of SkyDrive is somewhat less user friendly than Dropbox and Google Drive.

Advantages of Cloud Storage

•Usability - Every Cloud storage service listed here is easy to use and is accessible on easy-to-get devices like PCs, Tablets Androids etc.

•Bandwidth - As opposed to the traditional methods of sharing documents singly via email, you can upload it once to the Cloud storage and then share the links to all proposed recipients.